a SAVOR THE SOUTH® *cookbook*

Beans & Field Peas

SAVOR THE SOUTH® *cookbooks*

Beans and Field Peas, by Sandra A. Gutierrez
Sunday Dinner, by Bridgette A. Lacy
Crabs and Oysters, by Bill Smith
Gumbo, by Dale Curry (2015)
Shrimp, by Jay Pierce (2015)
Catfish, by Paul and Angela Knipple (2015)
Sweet Potatoes, by April McGreger (2014)
Southern Holidays, by Debbie Moose (2014)
Okra, by Virginia Willis (2014)
Pickles and Preserves, by Andrea Weigl (2014)
Bourbon, by Kathleen Purvis (2013)
Biscuits, by Belinda Ellis (2013)
Tomatoes, by Miriam Rubin (2013)
Peaches, by Kelly Alexander (2013)
Pecans, by Kathleen Purvis (2012)
Buttermilk, by Debbie Moose (2012)

a SAVOR THE SOUTH® *cookbook*

Beans & Field Peas

SANDRA A. GUTIERREZ

The University of North Carolina Press CHAPEL HILL

Library of Congress Cataloging-in-Publication Data
Gutierrez, Sandra A.
Beans and field peas / Sandra A. Gutierrez.
pages cm. — (A Savor the South cookbook)
Includes index.
ISBN 978-1-4696-2395-5 (cloth : alk. paper)
ISBN 978-1-4696-2396-2 (ebook)
1. Cooking (Beans) 2. Cooking, American—Southern style. I. Title.
TX803.B4G88 2015   641.6′565—dc23
2014048326

Contents

SIDEBARS

a SAVOR THE SOUTH® *cookbook*

Beans & Field Peas

Introduction

The sun was shining brightly outside, but from the ground right
up beside his window there was growing a great beanstalk, which
stretched up and up as far as he could see, into the sky.

—*from* Jack and the Beanstalk

Growing up in Latin America, from an early age, I was nourished with all kinds of delicious bean dishes. Refried beans may be the most recognized Latin American bean recipe in North America, but there are hundreds, if not thousands, of culinary formulas that feature beans in Latin America, not to mention throughout the world. Whether they were black, white, red, or speckled, beans made an appearance on my childhood's family table in Guatemala almost daily, sometimes refried but more often transformed into soups or stews, put into salads, or cooked with rice.

And today, as a cook and cookbook writer in my longtime home state of North Carolina, I've discovered the South's equal affinity for beans. I always find ways to incorporate legumes into my family's daily diet, not necessarily because they're healthy fare (which they are, but we'll get to that later) but because I just love eating them. I remember places I've visited by the food I ate, and so many fantastic bean dishes come to mind: the first time I had minestrone, chock-full of red beans, in a restaurant in Rome; my first bite of a *salade Niçoise* featuring tender haricots verts at a beach in the French Riviera; my first bowl of Cuban black beans and rice in Miami; that bowl o' red in Houston; and the cup of beans and rice I tasted in Mississippi.

While I didn't grow up on a family porch hulling peas, I have spent many hours in my North Carolina kitchen shelling them by the bushel, cooking them, and relishing their taste. Over the years, I've fallen in love with the food of the South and learned about its deep history and cultural nuances. Here, for example, I discovered that southerners cook their green beans long and

1

slowly—mostly because certain varieties require it and can't be eaten al dente—and that with delicious frequency, a few potatoes and some part of a hog will make it into the pot with them.

And then one day I discovered the fascinating realm of field peas. I had already encountered plenty of them in Latin American recipes (such as the *gandúles*, or pigeon peas, in Puerto Rican cuisine) and had eaten my share of black-eyed peas transformed into fritters. I knew well enough that the liquid left over from cooking beans and peas—called likker or pot likker in the South and *caldos* in Latin America—was something to be revered. Yet while it was sprinkled with toasted croutons in my family home, I learned the southern way of eating it—with buttermilk and cornbread. But the wide array of southern peas and their many southern-style preparations were novelties to me. That was a lip-smacking revelation indeed.

Beans and field peas are both legumes and seeds/beans that grow in pods. Beans are always dried before and cooked before they're eaten. Field peas, on the other hand, can be dried or eaten fresh. Green beans are also legumes and pods filled with immature beans, but the pods, of course, are eaten along with the beans. If you slice a green bean in half lengthwise, you'll see the immature beans inside; and if you've ever eaten a bowl of cooked half runners, you've probably enjoyed, as have I, finding the tiny, perfectly spherical white beans that escaped their edible green pods as they simmered. As you will see, all of these legumes have different uses in southern food.

Take some beans or peas, a touch of salt, a bit of fat (which in the South is often a piece of fatback, a slab of bacon, or a chunky ham hock), and a good amount of liquid (usually water), and you'll end up with a delicious pot of something good. That's all most legumes require to garner luscious flavor in the South.

Many people around the world eat a diet based on grains and legumes for economic reasons. So when in the 1990s it became popular to refer to recipes that were inexpensive and comforting—many of which were made of beans—as "cucina povera" or "peasant food," I found it interesting that what had forever been part of a way of life for many was now considered trendy.

For generations, beans and peas have graced the tables of southerners, but indigenous peoples of the world have subsisted on diets based on legumes for even longer. Throughout history, beans have provided nutrients and protein to millions of people who couldn't get them from other sources, such as meat, simply because they're not available to them or they can't afford them. Whether it is Brazil, Africa, or Italy, historically, beans have been the food of the poor. And they still are. That much hasn't changed. Recently, however, beans have broken through class barriers. Now, everyone eats beans. They're the culinary equalizer.

Here in the South, it was the same, historically speaking. The poorest people, among them enslaved African Americans, subsisted on mainly peas, beans, grains, and the rare piece of meat, usually the parts of animals that the wealthy considered inedible. However, in the South, beans and field peas quickly crossed over economic divisions. African slaves, who often were in charge of farm and plantation kitchens, greatly influenced the foodways of the South by introducing a harvest of beans and peas into the daily diets of the wealthy families who enslaved them.

George Washington is credited with importing field peas to Virginia when he brought forty bushels of seeds to sow on his own land in 1797. Another aristocrat who planted and ate peas was America's first epicure, Thomas Jefferson. In his *Farm Book*, Jefferson mentions planting and eating peas as early as 1767. In one entry on growing cowpeas at Monticello, dated 1771, Jefferson gives instructions on planting and rotating crops: "June is the proper time for planting peas, at which time, where they are to be mixed with corn, the corn may have been plowed 3 times." In his *Garden Book*, one entry reads: "Sowed patch of peas for the Fall [and] planted snap-beans." In another entry, he reports that he was planting and eating black-eyed peas and lima beans, writing that "black eye peas come to table." Heirloom peas are making a comeback in the South, brought to menus by chefs and farmers eager to rescue culinary traditions. Suddenly, today the food of the poor is also the food of those who embrace the finest regional cooking.

Vegetarianism may have taken the United States by storm during the 1960s, when beans were getting a second look as a nutritious alternative to meat, but in the South, beans and peas have always been a staple of ordinary life, making their daily appearance on the dining room sideboards of large estates, at the family tables on farms or in suburban homes, or at the lunch counters of small-town diners. They remain a key component of southern cuisine and are inextricably tied to southern food identity. Today we also celebrate the health benefits of eating a diet rich in legumes. They contain lots of cholesterol-lowering soluble fiber, are rich in potassium and folic acid, and are full of vitamins A, B, and D.

Let's look at the main types of beans and peas featured in this cookbook. From beans and green beans to cowpeas and black-eyed peas, from crowders and creamers to field peas and limas, a delicious world of healthful good eating opens here to everyone.

Beans

I was determined to know beans.
—*Henry David Thoreau*

The word "legume" means "true pod," and it derives from the Latin *legere*, to gather. Pods are nature's envelopes, little packages that protect a plant's seeds as they grow and mature. The beans are the mature seeds. Some pods are edible, while others are not; green beans are immature pods, filled with tiny seeds that are completely edible. The word *phaseolus* was used by Europeans to describe all beans (the Spanish word "frijoles" is the closest derivative of the original Latin term).

Early American civilizations from the Andes all the way up to North America cultivated beans alongside corn and squash, forming a trinity known by Native Americans as the "Three Sisters." The stalks of corn provided the poles on which bean stalks could grow, and the squash covered the ground with a thick blanket that kept the soil moist and free of weeds. Without the beans, however, the other two "sisters" wouldn't have survived, as the beans enriched the soil with nutrients (nitrogen, in particular) and regenerated it so that all three plants could thrive. Not surprisingly, squash, corn, and beans are still staples of the American diet, particularly in the South.

By the time European explorers arrived in North America, beans were already an integral part of the Native American diet. One of the first dishes settlers encountered in North America was succotash, a mixture of corn, beans, and squash. Not only did beans provide the protein people needed to subsist and flourish in the New World, but they also supplied the ground with the nitrogen that allowed corn to grow. Thus, although history has long given corn, with its tall and erect shafts, the most important place in the hierarchy of plants found in the Americas, one must wonder if the more whimsical beans, with their topsy-turvy vines, are the true backbone of the food pyramid of the New World.

All beans, including green beans, string beans, haricots verts, favas, and flageolets, belong to the same genus, *Phaseolus*, which is hard to believe given how different they all look. Southern peas, on the other hand, are members of the *Vigna* genus, which includes black-eyed peas, have Asian and African origins, and have nothing to do with beans.

In the South, vegetables and legumes have always been an integral part of a meal offering, whether the occasion calls for simply putting something nutritious and economical on the table or for serving a festive spread of edible offerings. The late John Egerton put this best in his book *Southern Food at Home, on the Road, in History*: "Living as they have so close to the gardens and fields, Southerners have maintained a fondness for vegetables through good times and bad." Every region of the South has its most popular varieties, so depending of where you live and what you grew up eating, those may include pinto, black, white, red, kidney, Calico, navy, or the great white northern.

Southerners will often lunch or dine on vegetable platters comprised of several kinds of vegetables and legumes. They can include a macaroni and cheese (which is considered a vegetable in the South!), boiled potatoes, buttery corn, stewed collard greens, fried okra, or sliced tomatoes, and beans or peas, of course. Meat often serves as the seasoning for any of these, be it a piece of ham that's shredded into a pot of pole beans or a bit of pork fat cooked with peas. No matter what the southern cook puts on a vegetable platter, though, it will almost always include one kind of pea or bean.

Green Beans

I grew up eating all kinds of green beans. I also learned to string them, to slice them thinly (sometimes diagonally in the French way), to cook them so that they retained their bright green color (with a pinch of baking soda in the water), to pickle them in escabeches, and to batter and fry them. There are many varieties of green beans: thin and elegant haricots verts, fat pole beans, snap beans, string beans that have to be cooked for a long time to become edible, and of course, the most common, Blue Lakes (which are not native to the South; developed commercially in the western United States in the early twentieth century, these crispy beans are uniform in size, hollow—that is, have no beans inside—and stringless).

In the South, green beans mean heirlooms like Kentucky Wonders, white or green half runners, greasy beans (so called because their pods shine as if they'd been greased), pole beans, and cutshorts (which have squared-off seeds because of overcrowding in the pod). According to my friend Ronni Lundy, an expert on southern foodways (particularly those of the mountain region of the South) and the author of *Butterbeans to Blackberries*, while green beans have remained a vegetable to serve as a side dish or as a component of a salad in other places, they're still an important element of the revered vegetable platter in the South. Green beans are lauded not for their crispness or bright green color but for their plumpness, a sure sign of the protein-filled beans within that offer both additional flavor and contrasting texture to their edible pods.

There are pole beans and bush beans. The first grow vertically and are easy to harvest. They're favored where space is an issue—as is the case in the mountain region of the South. Bush beans grow on vast bushes and require more space. According to Lundy, southerners prefer pole beans because they "deliver meatier, tastier beans than bush; and beans that have strings will taste better."

Bill Best, author of *Saving Seeds, Preserving Taste,* has hundreds of distinct heirloom green bean varieties in his seed stock; he's collected them from growers who have passed them down across generations. If you're looking for heirloom southern green beans your best bet is to shop seasonally at farmers' markets. Of course, you can always grow them yourself!

There is no comparison between the commercially produced beans found in most supermarkets today, which taste grassy, and the flavorful, buttery, farm or homegrown green beans of the South; the first taste mundane, while the latter taste of tradition.

Peas

How luscious lies the pea within the pod.
—*Emily Dickinson*

How beautiful also are the pods of southern peas that grow in shades of greens and purples, some variegated and others solidly colored. What first comes to mind at the mention of peas are the spherical green peas, or "English peas"—as southerners call them—sold at farmers' markets in the late spring. However, what southerners mean when they talk about eating peas are field peas. Whether fresh or dried, peas cook up just like beans do: to a soft, comforting consistency. Some of them have a starchier bite than others; dried ones benefit from a brief soaking before they're cooked.

There are more varieties of field peas than I could have ever imagined. It took me a long time to figure out that a "mess of peas" means a whole lot of them (enough to feed however many are assembled at a table), cooked together in a pot, sometimes with a few okra pods but almost always with a bit of "seasoning" (usually in the form of a slice of ham or a slab of bacon). Cooking peas and baking biscuits have a lot more in common than you might think: you've got to do both well in order to pass muster as a southern cook. Before shelling machines came along, field peas had to be shelled by hand, a tedious chore that often led to sore fingers. Today, there are shelling machines that keep fingers from getting bruised, and farmers offer them packed neatly in bags at the market. Some peas can be found frozen in grocery stores that cater to a southern clientele.

The word "pea" comes from the Latin *pisum*, which derives from the Greek word *pison*. The Old English changed it to *pise* (later *pease*), which ultimately became "peas." Peas belong to the *Vigna unguiculata* species in the *Fabaceae* family, and they have been feeding humankind for a very long time. Peas were cultivated and eaten by the ancient Egyptians, Greeks, and Romans. It appears that people have been pairing peas and pork for just as long. The historian Maguelonne Toussaint-Samat wrote that Romans ate dried peas and that the French Renaissance humanist François Rabelais "enjoyed dried peas cooked with a good piece of bacon" in the 1500s.

In the colonial southern United States, butter beans reminded early settlers of English peas (which they couldn't grow easily in the South); eventually, all legumes came to be known as southern peas. They came in all colors, shapes, and sizes; some resembled small beads, some were large and flat, others were kidney-shaped, and still others were coquettishly speckled. Thomas Harriot, an English diarist who accompanied one of the first expeditions to the Americas, described how these became known as peas in his book *A Brief and True Report of the New Founde Lande of Virginia*: "We named them peas to distinguish them from the beans, because they are much smaller . . . though they are far better than our English peas."

Harriot was likely describing butter beans, which are native to North America (cowpeas had not yet made it to this side of the world). Harriot also gave an account of the Native Americans he encountered, describing in one instance the way they prepare peas: "Peas are either cooked by themselves or mixed with wheat [corn]. Sometimes after they have been boiled whole they are pounded in a mortar and made into loaves or lumps of doughy bread." The first dish he was referring to was probably succotash (from the Narragansett word *sukquttahash*).

In the South, peas are typically divided into four major groups: black-eyed peas (or cowpeas), crowder peas, creamers, and field peas, and there are hundreds of varieties within each of these categories. However, trying to keep the names of all of the different varieties of peas straight is a gargantuan task. Indeed, it's almost impossible, because, since colonial times, southerners have used the words "peas," "cowpeas" and "field peas" interchangeably, regardless of what kind of peas they are actually describing. Adding to the confusion is the fact that even experts on peas, scholars, and southern authors, can't agree on how to spell these, so while some spell them as "butterbeans" or "cowpeas," others spell them as two separate words (i.e., butter beans, cow peas, etc.). I've chosen to spell them one way (which may stir the pot of controversy on a subject that is still filled with gray areas) for the purposes of consistency throughout this book. Zippers, ruckers, turkey craws, Emily Lees, rattlesnakes, whippoorwills, Dixie Lees, lady peas, colossus, big red ripper, calico crowder, pink-eyed, purple hulls, and Mississippi silvers are just a few of the names of the many pea varieties out there. But don't let this list overwhelm you! The area in which you live will most likely dictate the varieties that are available to you. Here, I'll guide you through some of the most popular and easily found field peas in the South.

Cowpeas and Black-Eyed Peas

The cultivation of black-eye peas (*Vigna unguiculata*) dates back 6,000 years to Africa, where they are believed to have originated and where they were planted alongside sorghum and millet. In his book *Beans: A History*, Ken Albala writes that "peas were probably one of the earliest domesticated plants along with wheat and barley, archaeological remains of which date back as far as 8000 BCE."

Black-eyed peas are also called cowpeas (*caupí* or *caupíes* in Spanish- and Portuguese-speaking countries and the Caribbean). The etymology of the term "cowpea" is unclear. Dr. David Shields, a professor at the University of South Carolina and the chairman of the Carolina Gold Society, believes that the term "cowpeas" first appeared in South Carolina newspapers as far back as the 1780s. It is commonly believed, he says, that cowpeas, in the South at least, were so named because pea hay and the vines left after harvesting were fed to cattle. However, we also agreed that this is still not yet fully proven.

It would be impossible to write about black-eyed peas without mentioning their importance in African American foodways. Black-eyed peas were brought from West Africa to the New World by human traffickers in the same ships that carried the enslaved during the African diaspora, and they are known to have arrived in Jamaica around 1675. The peas provided at least one familiar source of food for enslaved Africans in the New World. By the 1700s, black-eyed peas were widely cultivated in Florida and North Carolina. Today, Africa still produces the majority of the world supply of black-eyed peas. In *Beans*, Albala writes, "We often have this image of slaves secreting their favorite seeds in their pockets before being forced across the Atlantic. Even if a few stray beans arrived this way, more likely slave owners began to import African crops after their captives refused to eat."

Jessica B. Harris, in her great book *High on the Hog*, also argues that wherever enslaved Africans were taken, so went peas, millet, rice, okra, and other foods from West Africa—all ingredients that are now recognized as the foods of the African diaspora and that proud African Americans in the 1970s reclaimed as their own and came to celebrate at their tables.

When peas arrived in the South, they thrived in southern soil. The weather conditions were ideal for their harvest, and since peas were able to withstand tropical environments and grow without much help, they fared well even during the hot and humid southern summers. The seeds of open pollinator plants could be saved and planted year after year (heirloom peas are still produced this way). The plants had a long life span, producing peas for four to six months—which allowed enslaved workers, who often grew them in the small garden plots allotted to them, to supplement their meager rations.

In kitchens across the South, enslaved Africans cooked the foods that were familiar to them using traditional West African methods. In her book *The Virginia House-Wife*, Mary Randolph includes a recipe for black-eyed pea "fried cakes," which are similar to the fritters (or *acarás*) that are still cooked in West Africa.

Black-eyed peas are just one of the many ingredients (among them okra, rice, and sorghum) that united the foodways of Africa and the American South, in some ways bridging the divide between races and classes. Harris put it best when she wrote: "In the kitchens, African hands also prevailed, and for generations, whether in plantation kitchens or in-town backyards, they turned the wooden spoons in the pots."

Those of us who live in the South know that black-eyed peas are supposed to bring good luck. In *High on the Hog* Harris reveals that the belief originated in Africa. Food has a way of connecting us to our roots; it brings a sense of comfort and gives identity to its people, through space and time. Few southerners would consider tempting fate on New Year's Day by not eating black-eyed peas!

The most common black-eyed peas are white and flecked with—of course—black eyes. Other varieties, however, come in different colors: pink-eyed, red-eyed, six-week brown-eyed, and my favorite, because they retain their color through cooking, yellow-eyed. Of these, the pink-eyed and black-eyed peas produce the darkest broth, called pot likker, which is often served with cornbread and a glass of buttermilk.

Crowder Peas

Crowder peas (which southerners sometimes also call cowpeas) grow in a tight row in the pod, so tight, in fact, that the seeds become almost square or tapered at the ends. All crowders become soft and creamy when cooked. They are the starchiest of the peas and produce a rich, dark pot likker. Brown crowders produce the darkest pot likker of them all.

Purple hulls are a popular crowder variety. The colorful pods that range from a vibrant violet to a mottled purplish green, offer peas that become soft when cooked. As do other colorful peas, these light-green peas with purple eyes, lose their hue as they cook, turning dark brown. In the process they produce a succulent, medium-dark likker. Some cooks add a touch of bacon fat to the simmering peas, but others simply cook them in water, toss them with sweet butter, and serve them in little bowls with their likker.

There are many varieties of crowder peas, but some of the most popular include whippoorwills, white sumptuous, blue goose, brown sugar, dimpled brown southern, early Scarlett, and calico.

Creamer Peas

Creamers are prized for their velvety and buttery texture and are usually light in color (they vary from a white, to a slightly yellow, to a light green). Butter beans belong in this category (although, as I explain below, they're not truly peas but beans, members of the *Sieva* family). Sweet lady creamers, which resemble corn kernels, are considered by many to be the princesses among the peas. They produce a delicate, clear pot likker and are prized for their flavor. Other popular varieties are the Texas white, white acre southern, red ripper southern, and speckled butter bean. Speckled butter beans, which are flat and shaped like lima beans and have pinkish specks, are very popular where I live.

Field Peas

Now they knew that she was a real princess because she had felt the pea right through the twenty mattresses and the twenty eider-down beds. Nobody but a real princess could be as sensitive as that.
—*from Hans Christian Anderson,* The Princess and the Pea

Field peas are the smallest of all the peas. The smooth Dixie Lees are perhaps the most common. When they're fresh, they're light green or yellow, a beautiful sight when shelled into a bowl, but once dried, they turn a dark brown and produce a very dark pot likker when cooked. Dixie Lees, and the lighter brown lady peas, are abundant in North Carolina in late June and early July. They're delicious served over rice, with a cleanly flavored corn and tomato salad.

Lima Beans

Lima beans belong to the *Phaseolus lunatus* family, also native to the Americas. Limas were first domesticated in Peru (hence their name) and are a different species altogether than peas. Butter beans are a subspecies of lima beans called *Sieva*, first domesticated in Central America and often called baby limas in the South. They're smaller than lima beans and a brighter shade of green. Butter beans are also considered to be crowders. In the South, you'll find both green and white lima beans.

A Seasonal Gift

In the South, depending on the variety, peas plants generally start making an appearance in late June and last through the end of October. They produce peas over a four- to six-month period. The immature pods, or "snaps," can be eaten raw in salads; the just-plump pods, filled with rows of tender peas, are the best kind for freezing and need only be cooked lightly; and the pods with peas that have begun to dry can be harvested and cooked. Luckily, most peas can be shelled and frozen so that we can enjoy them well after the cicadas have sung their last summer tune and after the first frost has kissed the ground.

No matter which peas you cook, mix enough of them in a pot and you'll end up with a delicious mess of peas. Or cook them with corn, summer squash, and peppers and make yourself a bowl of succotash. Enjoy these classic, contemporary, and international recipes and have fun discovering the universe of southern peas. In every season, you'll always be prepared with plenty at hand. And don't forget to welcome each New Year with a potful of luck.

Classic Southern Dishes

For generations, southern cooks have lovingly prepared beans and field peas in their kitchens. In the South, bean and pea recipes are simple and unassuming, but they produce comforting flavor and great sustenance and are utterly delicious. Southerners who are able to raise their own beans and peas benefit from a larger variety than what most of us can get in our markets. However, as the farm-to-fork movement has taken off, more consumers are demanding the return of the heirloom varieties of beans and peas that commercial producers have ignored for a long time. In the meantime, farmers' market or roadside farm stands are a good source for them. If you're craving these dishes out of season, though, look to the frozen section of your grocery stores; they usually carry a variety of good-quality beans and peas. But no matter what kind of beans or peas you're in the mood for or the season offers, here you'll learn how to cook them so they garner scrumptious flavor. From relishes and salads, to main dishes and desserts, here are the classics.

FRED SAUCEMAN'S LEATHER BRITCHES

My friend Fred Sauceman, an esteemed author and a professor at East Tennessee State University, is an expert on the foodways of the Appalachian region and the American South, I am lucky and grateful that he has shared the following essay on leather britches for inclusion in this book. Newcomers to the South may have never come across the dried beans found in the Appalachian region. More than a recipe, this is his description of the method used for drying the green beans. Here it is demystified, in Fred's own words:

Before the era of refrigeration and before the development of canning techniques, Native Americans and early settlers relied heavily on drying in order to make the bounty of the garden last through the fall and winter months. Dried, whole beans were referred to as shuck beans, shucky beans, and leather britches in America's Appalachian region. The entire hull is dried, not just the bean itself. The drying not only preserves the bean, but it also intensifies the flavor once it is reconstituted in water.

Modern-day commercial green beans generally cannot be preserved, at least in an edible way, by drying, because plant breeding has toughened their skins. Heirloom varieties, such as cut-shorts and greasy beans, are best for drying.

With a pair of scissors, snip off the stem ends of each bean. Then, thread a darning needle with white string, such as kite string. Pass the needle and string all the way through the center of a bean and then loop the string around that bean and tie it, to prevent the beans from coming off the string. Continue until your string is full, leaving a little space between each bean. Make a loop on the end of the string and hang the beans on a wire in a dry place. A typical kitchen is fine. Leave the beans as they are for about a month. Part of the appeal of leather britches is the rattle the dried bean pods make when touched.

After the month is up, either cook the beans or store them in a covered container or in the freezer.

To cook them, rinse and drain the beans several times. Place them in a bowl and cover them with water. Let the beans sit overnight—for about 12 hours. Change the water at least a couple of times. Drain the beans a final time and put them in a pot. Cover them with water and add a ham hock and an onion, quartered. Bring to a boil. Then reduce the heat and cook for about half a day, adding more water when necessary. When the ham hock is done and the meat begins to fall off the bone, take the hock out of the pot, let it cool, remove the meat, break it into small pieces, and return the cleaned meat to the pot. When the beans are tender, season them with salt and pepper. If you want the beans soupy, keep the broth in the pot. If you want to serve them in the same manner as regular green beans, cook out most of the liquid.

Author's Note: Make sure to remove the strings of the beans before you begin the process. To do this, simply pull the ends of the beans lengthwise on each direction until the string is removed.

Red Beans and Rice

This is the classic combination of rice and beans that you'll find in Louisiana and Mississippi. It features the Cajun flavor base composed of onion, bell pepper, and celery, known as the holy trinity. I will never forget dining at the Ajax Diner in Oxford, Mississippi, on a rainy day in October and relishing every last bite of this southern stick-to-your-ribs favorite. When I returned home from my trip, I got busy trying to create my own version. The ham and sausage will add salt to the dish so don't be tempted to add salt before the recipe is fully finished. I like to serve this as part of a vegetable platter that includes long-cooked green beans, sliced tomatoes, and squash casserole.

MAKES 6–8 SERVINGS

1 pound dried red beans, cleaned of debris

1 (12-ounce) chunk country ham or tasso ham

2 tablespoons vegetable oil

1 cup finely chopped yellow onion

1 cup finely chopped green bell pepper

1 cup finely chopped celery

8 ounces andouille sausage, roughly chopped

2 bay leaves

1 teaspoon thyme

1 teaspoon cayenne pepper

2 garlic cloves, finely minced

Salt and freshly ground black pepper, to taste

6 cups cooked long-grain white rice

Hot sauce, to taste

Place the beans in a large bowl and add enough cold water to cover them by 2 inches; soak them for at least 6 hours or overnight (or use my quick-soak method, page 32). Drain the beans and rinse them under cold water.

Place the beans and ham in a large Dutch oven; add enough cold water to cover by at least 1 inch. Bring to a boil over medium-high heat; cover, reduce the heat, and simmer for 45 minutes or until the beans are soft but still mealy. Add more water if necessary (you should always have at least 1 inch of liquid above the beans). Remove the ham and set aside to cool.

In a medium-size skillet, heat the oil over medium heat. Add the onion, bell pepper, and celery, stirring until softened, about 4–5 minutes. Add the andouille, bay leaves, thyme, and cayenne. Cook for 2–3 minutes or until the andouille is cooked through; stir in the garlic and cook for 30 seconds or until fragrant. Remove from the heat and add this mixture to the beans.

Chop the ham into bite-size pieces and return to the pot of beans; continue simmering for 40–45 minutes or until the beans have softened. Remove the bay leaves. Season with salt and pepper.

Ladle the rice into bowls and top with the bean mixture. Serve with a splash of hot sauce.

Drunken Beans

In Spanish, these pinto beans are known as frijoles borrachos *because they're cooked in beer. If you've never tried them before, you'll be surprised by their subtly sweet and smoky flavor. This recipe is very common along the U.S. border with Mexico, and you'll find variations on the theme all the way from New Mexico to Texas. I recommend that you use your favorite Mexican beer because you'll be able to taste it throughout the dish. I like these beans on the soupy side, but if you prefer them a bit thicker, remove and mash some of the beans and return them to the pot. Serve them on their own, with flour tortillas, or as a side dish with grilled meats.*

MAKES 6 SERVINGS

½ pound dried pinto beans, cleaned of debris

3 cups beer (preferably Mexican)

4 ounces chopped country ham

2 cups chopped yellow onion

6 large garlic cloves, minced

1½ to 2 teaspoons salt, or to taste

Place the beans in a large bowl. Add enough water to cover the beans by at least 2 inches; soak them for at least 6 hours or overnight (or use my quick-soak method, page 32). Drain the beans and rinse them under cold water.

Place the beans in an 8-quart pot; add the beer and enough water to cover the beans by 2 inches. Add the ham, onion, and garlic and bring the beans to a boil over medium-high heat; partially cover the pot with a lid, reduce the heat to low, and simmer the beans slowly until they've softened, about 2–2½ hours. Add more water if necessary (you should always have at least 1 inch of liquid above the beans); season with salt.

If you wish them to be thicker, remove 1 cup of the cooked beans from the pot; mash them well with a fork and return them to the pot. Simmer for 5 additional minutes and serve.

Crock Pot Pinto Beans

Everyone should have at least one crock pot recipe for beans, and this is a great one. I'll never forget the first time I met Miss Mildred Council at an author presentation in Durham. Her sweet character and depth of spirit moved me. Like many, I became enamored of her story and of her cookbook, which went on to become a best-seller. Throughout the years, I've had the pleasure of talking to Miss Council many times and to hearing her talk about her life. Her restaurant, Mama Dip's, is an institution in Chapel Hill. I like to take out-of-town guests there so they can savor an authentic southern meal. This is her recipe, and I'm delighted to include it here. I cook these anywhere from 6 to 8 hours in my slow cooker on low. If this is your first time cooking beans in a slow cooker, begin checking them after 6 hours (some beans will soften quicker than others).

MAKES 6 SERVINGS

1 pound dried pinto beans, cleaned of debris
2 teaspoons garlic salt
1/2 cup chopped onion
Ham hock, butter, or margarine

Wash the beans in warm water. Whisk to remove grit and then drain the beans. Put the beans in a small pot with water to cover and boil for 20 minutes. Drain the beans and put in a crock pot with the garlic salt, onion, ham hock (or butter or margarine), and enough water to cover by 2 inches. Cook until the beans are tender, adding a little hot water if needed.

From *Mama Dip's Family Cookbook*, by Mildred Council. © 2005 Mildred Council. Used by permission of the University of North Carolina Press.

Ranch-Style Beans
Frijoles Charros

Pinto beans take a spicy and smoky bath in liquid that's flavored with bacon and chiles. Charro *means "rancher" in Spanish. This is another favorite way to prepare beans along the Texas/Mexican border and in northern Mexico. I like the taste imparted by fire-roasted tomatoes, which enhance the smokiness already in the recipe. If you can't find fire-roasted tomatoes, you can use regular ones. Serve these beans in bowls with plenty of liquid—they're meant to be soupy. Like many bean dishes, this one tastes even better a day after it's made, but because I'm always eager to eat them, I make a double batch, eat half immediately, and save the rest for later. These beans freeze beautifully, for up to 4 months.*

MAKES 6–8 SERVINGS

½ pound dried pinto beans, cleaned of debris

4 cups chicken broth

2 bay leaves

4 ounces bacon, chopped

1½ cups chopped yellow onion

5 large garlic cloves, chopped

3 serrano chiles, thinly sliced (seeded and deveined for
    less heat, if desired)

1 (14.5 ounce) can diced fire-roasted tomatoes
    (or regular tomatoes)

1½–2 teaspoons salt, or to taste

¼ cup finely chopped cilantro (leaves and tender stems)

¼ cup thinly sliced green onions

Place the beans in a large bowl. Add enough water to cover the beans by at least 2 inches; soak them for at least 6 hours or overnight (or use my quick-soak method, page 32). Drain the beans and rinse them under cold water.

Place the beans in an 8-quart pot, add the broth, the bay leaves, and enough water to cover the beans by 2 inches. Bring to a boil over medium-high heat; partially cover the pot with a lid, reduce the heat to low and simmer the beans slowly until they've softened, about 2–2½ hours. If necessary, add more water (you should always have at least 1 inch of liquid above the beans).

In a medium skillet set over medium heat, cook the bacon until it is beginning to crisp, about 3–4 minutes. Add the onions, garlic, and chiles and cook until the onions have softened, about 2–3 minutes. Stir in the tomatoes, reduce the heat to low, and simmer for 5 minutes. Stir this mixture into the beans and simmer, partially covered, for 10 minutes. Remove the bay leaves; season with salt and ladle into bowls. Sprinkle with the cilantro and green onions.

White Bean and Chicken Chili

When I was young, my family traveled to Texas on a regular basis, and that's where I first tasted the stew made with beef and red chiles and learned that a traditional "bowl o' red" never contains beans or tomatoes. However, I also encountered a different kind of chili: one that was chock-full of white beans, rich in chicken flavor, bursting with tomatillos, and enhanced with green chiles. When given the choice, I always chose the white variation over the red one. Upon my arrival to North Carolina, I was pleased to find that this spicy stew was very popular with home cooks. I had plenty of bowls both at the now-defunct Coyote Café in Cary and at many of our friends' homes around the Triangle. It didn't take me long to create my own version of this recipe. I prefer to use dried white beans, but here is a recipe where canned beans can easily be substituted without any loss of flavor, as long as they are rinsed before they're added to the pot. If you use canned beans, cut the cooking time in half, or they'll get too soft.

MAKES 6–8 SERVINGS

1 pound cooked white beans (navy, white, or great northern)
8 Anaheim peppers, roasted, peeled, seeded, and deveined
1 cup minced white onion
12 medium tomatillos, husks removed, rinsed and quartered
2 jalapeño peppers, coarsely chopped (seeded and deveined
　　for less heat)
2 garlic cloves
1 cup cilantro (leaves and tender stems), packed
2 teaspoons salt, plus more, to taste
1½ teaspoons ground cumin
1 teaspoon ground coriander
1½–2 cups chicken broth
2 tablespoons vegetable oil

1 pound boneless, skinless chicken thighs, cut into small cubes
1 cup sour cream
2 cups shredded Monterey Jack cheese

In a blender, combine the Anaheim peppers, onion, tomatillos, jalapeños, garlic, cilantro, salt, cumin, and coriander; add enough broth to get the motor started and purée until smooth.

Heat the oil in a 6- to 8-quart Dutch oven over medium heat; add the chicken and cook, stirring, until the chicken is no longer pink, about 2–3 minutes. Stir in the puréed mixture and bring to a boil, stirring occasionally, about 3–4 minutes. Add the beans and the remaining broth and bring to a boil; reduce the heat and simmer for 40–45 minutes. Season with salt and ladle into bowls; serve hot, topped with a dollop of sour cream and a generous amount of cheese.

Southern Baked Beans

*Great northern beans are white and creamy, and in the South,
they are harvested in the spring; they're dried and then sold at the
start of summer. In the South, you'll find many renditions of this
dish made up of soft, baked beans, cooked in a tomato-enhanced
sauce that is thickened and sweetened with sorghum. While molasses is extracted from sugarcane, sorghum is obtained from the*
sorghum bicolor *plant, a type of grass with tall stalks that are
pressed until their clear liquid is extracted. The juices are cooked
and reduced into thick, amber-colored syrup that has a milder
taste than molasses. You can substitute molasses here, but keep in
mind that the sauce will be a bit darker and thicker. This is a great
covered dish to share with a crowd.*

MAKES 10–12 SERVINGS

1 tablespoon vegetable oil

½ pound salt pork (side meat, fatback, or pork belly),
  chopped into small cubes

1 large white onion, finely chopped (about 2½ cups)

1 large green bell pepper, stemmed, seeded, and finely
  chopped (about 1½ cups)

4 large garlic cloves, minced

1 pound great northern beans, cooked and drained well

2 (28-ounce) cans diced tomatoes with juice

2 cups chicken broth

1 cup sorghum (or unsulfured molasses)

½ teaspoon freshly ground black pepper

Preheat the oven to 375°.

In a 6- to 8-quart oven-safe Dutch oven, combine the oil, salt pork, onion, bell pepper, and garlic. Cook, stirring, over medium-high heat until the onions have softened, about 4–5 minutes. Add the beans, tomatoes, broth, sorghum, and pepper, stirring until well combined. Remove the pan from the heat, cover tightly, and place it in the preheated oven. Bake for 2 hours or until the beans are fork-tender and the sauce has thickened.

Muslim Bean Pie

My dear friend Nancie McDermott, cookbook author extraordinaire and pie expert, introduced me to this classic southern pie, which has a sweet, thick, custardy filling that's absolutely addictive. According to Nancie, this pie originated with Elijah Muhammad, leader of the Nation of Islam from the 1930s to the 1970s. He considered sweet potatoes unhealthy (although he had no reason to believe so), and encouraged his followers to avoid them. He included a recipe for a bean pie that is similar to classic sweet potato pie in his writings. The pie has been a mainstay of African American home cooks and bakeries across the country since the 1930s. As Nancie put it, "This café-au-lait colored pie is uniquely delicious, and stands on its own as a dessert pleasure." I hope you'll try it and add it to your pie repertoire.

MAKES 6–8 SERVINGS

Pastry for a 9-inch single-crust pie

1 cup sugar

1 tablespoon all-purpose flour

½ teaspoon ground cinnamon

½ teaspoon grated nutmeg

½ cup evaporated milk (or half-and-half)

¼ cup butter (or margarine), melted

2 large eggs

1 tablespoon pure vanilla extract

1 cup homemade or canned cooked (drained and rinsed) navy beans, mashed (see Note)

Preheat the oven to 350°. Line a 9-inch pie pan with the pastry and crimp the edges decoratively.

In a medium bowl, place the sugar, flour, cinnamon, and nutmeg and stir with a fork to mix well. Add the milk, butter, eggs, and vanilla and mix well. Add the mashed beans and with a fork or a whisk, beat the ingredients together until thick and fairly smooth. Pour the filling into the piecrust.

Place the pie in the middle of the oven. Bake 45–55 minutes or until the filling puffs up and the center is fairly firm (it will barely wiggle when you gently nudge the pan). Place the pie on a cooling rack or a folded kitchen towel and cool for 20–30 minutes. Serve warm or at room temperature.

NOTE ❋ You can also use great northern, cannellini, or pinto beans in this recipe.

Nancie McDermott's Soup Bean Pie

Give all the credit to my friend Nancie McDermott, who is a treasured cookbook author and expert on southern pies, for sharing not one but two sweet pie recipes that feature beans. This one has its roots in the mountains of the American South, where beans play an important role on the everyday menu. Although pinto beans are usually cooked with pork and topped with raw onions, here they are transformed into a custardy and sweet filling scented with cinnamon and reminiscent of pumpkin pie. Bake it during the holidays, for church picnics, or just for the sake of it. In fact, bake two pies and share them with those you love.

MAKES 6–8 SERVINGS

Pastry for a 9-inch single-crust pie

½ cup granulated sugar

½ cup packed brown sugar

½ cup evaporated milk, half-and-half, or milk

½ cup butter, melted

2 eggs, beaten well

1 teaspoon pure vanilla extract

½ teaspoon ground cinnamon

¼ teaspoon salt

1½ cups home-cooked pinto beans or 1 (15-ounce) can
(drained and rinsed), mashed (see Note)

Preheat the oven to 375°. Line a 9-inch pie pan with the pastry and crimp the edges decoratively.

In a medium bowl, whisk together the sugar, brown sugar, milk, butter, eggs, vanilla, cinnamon, and salt. Add the beans to the milk mixture and mix well.

Pour the filling into the crust and place it on the middle rack of the oven. Bake for 10 minutes. Reduce the heat to 325° and bake until the filling is firm, puffed up, and handsomely browned, 35–45 minutes more. Place the pie on a cooling rack or on a folded kitchen towel and cool for at least 20 minutes. Serve warm or at room temperature.

NOTE ❋ You can use a food processor or blender to make a smooth purée or hand-mash them for a more rustic texture.

COOKING BEANS

Here are some tips for cooking the best beans possible:

* Leave plenty of time to soak the beans (at least 6 hours or overnight), which must be softened before they are cooked. (Although if you're in a hurry, you can use the quick-soak method described below.) The beans should be covered by at least 2 inches of cold water for soaking. After they've been soaked for the allotted time, drain and rinse the beans well.
* To quick-soak beans, place them in a large pan and add enough cold water to cover them by at least 2 inches; bring the water to a boil and cook the beans at a rolling boil for 2 minutes. Turn off the heat, cover the pan, and let them soak for 1 hour; drain and discard the liquid and continue with the recipe.
* Cook beans in plenty of water. They should be covered by at least 2 inches of water at all times during cooking.
* Don't add salt or acids (such as tomatoes, vinegar, or citrus) to the beans until they're fork-tender. If you add these too soon, some beans will not soften.
* Although the foam that rises to the top of the pan during the first few minutes of cooking beans doesn't affect their flavor, it does make the pot likker cloudy, so I prefer to remove the foam in some recipes.
* Older beans will take a longer time to cook than younger beans. Since there is no way of knowing how long beans have sat on store shelves before we purchase them, we have to judge the doneness of all beans as they cook. If you purchase your dried beans from a mail-order source such as Rancho Gordo or from your local farmers' markets or if you grow your own, they will likely cook faster than those purchased at grocery stores, where the beans don't sell quickly.

* The most important rule of thumb when it comes to beans is not to undercook them. An "al dente" texture is not what you want for beans. Cooked beans should be soft and creamy. To test for the doneness, I press a few beans between my fingers—if they mash easily, they're done; if they don't, I just let them cook longer and check them again later.
* The only thing worse than undercooked beans is burnt ones—trust me on this one. That's why beans are cooked for a long time at a very low temperature. It's easy to scorch beans at the bottom of a pot when the heat is too high.

Hoppin' John

In a scene in Carson McCuller's novel The Member of the Wedding, *the main character, F. Jasmine, expresses her love for this southern rice and pea dish. She exclaims that if she died and her friends needed proof that she was really dead, all they'd have to do was wave a plate of this dish before her nose. If she was alive, she would jump up and eat, but if she "did not stir, then they could just nail down the coffin and be certain she was truly dead." This recipe is indeed completely irresistible with its smoky bacon flavor and its spicy kick achieved by the addition of the ubiquitous southern pepper: cayenne. It's the perfect side dish for just about anything, but I fancy it best when it's served with a simple roast chicken.*

MAKES 6 SERVINGS

¼ pound bacon or smoked ham

½ cup finely chopped yellow onion

½ large green bell pepper, cored, seeded, and finely chopped (about ½ cup)

2 large garlic cloves, minced

1 cup long-grain rice

2 cups water

½ pound cooked black-eyed peas, cowpeas, or red peas (about 1½ cups)

⅛ teaspoon cayenne pepper

1 teaspoon salt

¼ teaspoon freshly ground black pepper

Place the bacon or smoked ham in a 3½- to 4-quart Dutch oven set over medium-high heat. Cook until the bacon renders and begins to brown and get crispy, about 3–4 minutes. Add the onion and bell pepper and cook, stirring, until they begin to soften, about 2½–3 minutes. Add the garlic and cook until fragrant, about 30 seconds. Add the rice and stir well to coat all the grains with oil, about 30 seconds. Add the water and stir, being sure to scrape up the brown bits at the bottom of the pan. Add the peas, cayenne, salt, and pepper. Bring to a boil; cover, reduce the heat to low, and simmer for 20–25 minutes or until all of the liquid has been absorbed.

Southern Caviar

This classic black-eyed pea salad is cooked all over the South, from Georgia to Tennessee, and all the way down to Texas. Most recipes, like this one, feature creamy peas infused with citrus, but this version has an added touch of heat, courtesy of a few hot peppers. Southern cooks usually serve it for New Year's celebrations because it is believed that black-eyed peas will bring good fortune for the year to come. The way I see it, a little bit of good luck comes in handy any time of the year, so I also make this salad during the summer months. I add chopped avocado whenever I have a ripe one in my kitchen.

MAKES 8 SERVINGS

4½ cups cooked black-eyed peas

1 cup finely chopped red bell pepper

1 cup seeded and finely chopped plum tomatoes

¾ cup finely chopped red onion

¼ cup finely chopped Italian parsley (leaves and tender stems)

2 tablespoons finely chopped jalapeño peppers
(seeded and deveined for less heat)

1 large garlic clove, minced

½ cup fresh lemon juice

2 teaspoons Dijon mustard

1½ teaspoon salt, or to taste

¼ teaspoon freshly ground black pepper

¼ teaspoon Worcestershire sauce

Pinch cayenne pepper, or to taste

¼ cup extra-virgin olive oil

In a large bowl, combine the black-eyed peas, bell pepper, tomatoes, onion, parsley, jalapeños, and garlic; stir until combined.

In a separate, medium bowl, whisk together the lemon juice, mustard, salt, pepper, Worcestershire sauce, and cayenne pepper. Slowly, while whisking, add the oil in a thin stream until combined.

Pour the dressing on the salad and stir to combine. Chill the salad for 30 minutes (or up to 24 hours) before serving.

Perre's Pickled Field Peas

This vibrant and tasty recipe comes from my good friend Perre Coleman Magness, a fabulous food writer and the voice behind the Runaway Spoon blog. Perre uses purple hull, pink-eye, or black eye peas because the darker peas, such as whippoorwill or crowder peas, will turn the brine an unattractive color. Consider doing as she does and make it entirely with black-eyed peas and give it to your friends as a New Year's good luck treat. Try to find peas that are uniform in size, so that they'll cook evenly. Serve this relish with corn chips, for dipping.

MAKES ABOUT 7 HALF-PINT JARS

2 pounds fresh purple hull, pink-eyed, or black-eyed peas
(or a combination)
1 large Vidalia onion, finely chopped
2 green bell peppers, cored, seeded, and finely chopped
1 red or orange bell pepper, cored, seeded, and finely chopped
3 large garlic cloves, minced
2 cups cider vinegar
1 cup sugar
4 tablespoons canning salt (or 3 tablespoons table salt)
$1\frac{1}{2}$ teaspoons dry mustard
1 teaspoon celery seed
1 teaspoon freshly ground black pepper
$\frac{1}{2}$ teaspoon sweet paprika

Place the peas in a large bowl, cover with cold water, and soak for about 10 minutes. Skim off any floating peas.

Using your hands, gently scoop the peas out of the water (leaving any dirt and debris behind) and place them in a 5-quart Dutch oven. Add enough water to cover the peas by 2 inches. Bring to a boil, reduce the heat, and simmer for 10 minutes, just until they start to soften (they should still have a bite to them).

Drain the peas and return them to the pot; add the onion, bell peppers, and garlic and stir well to combine. Add the vinegar and sugar and stir well; add the salt, mustard, celery seed, pepper, and paprika and bring to a boil over medium-high heat; reduce the heat to medium (or medium-low) and simmer gently for 10 minutes, stirring occasionally.

While the peas are cooking, boil water in a canner or large stockpot. When the peas are almost ready, pour some boiling water over the lids of the jars to soften the seals; set aside.

When the peas are cooked, immediately scoop them into the sterilized canning jars. Top each jar with a little extra brine to cover, leaving ¼ inch head space. Dry the lids with a clean paper towel and place them on the jars. Screw on the bands; then process the jars in the boiling water bath for 15 minutes. Refrigerate any extra peas (eat them within a week) and discard any extra brine. When the jars are processed, leave them to cool on a towel on the counter. The processed jars will keep for a year in a cool, dark place.

Pink-Eyed Peas, Corn, Tomato, and Bacon Salad

This salad is a beautiful kaleidoscope of colors with ingredients that are coated by deliciously tangy vinaigrette that lends a pleasant contrast of flavors. Pink-eyed peas are found in the late summer months. Look for them at your farmers' markets. These pretty peas are nestled in a neat row inside long, narrow pods that range in color from a light green with purple flecks to deep eggplant purple. I buy them by the bucketful and then enlist the help of my family to shell them. Once shelled, divide them into small batches; blanch and freeze them so that they'll last you a few months. There's nothing like eating peas long after the summer is over. When raw, these peas are crunchy, but once cooked, they become buttery and soft. Pink-eyed peas lose some of their pretty color when cooked but their flavor retains every bit of summer goodness.

MAKES 4–6 SERVINGS

6–8 slices of bacon (about 6 ounces)

3 cups fresh or frozen, shelled pink-eyed peas
   (about 1 pound unshelled)

2 cups fresh corn kernels (or frozen and thawed)

2 cups seeded and chopped tomatoes (any variety in season)

¼ cup finely chopped yellow or white onion

1 large garlic clove, minced

¼ cup plus 2 tablespoons apple cider or red wine vinegar

¼ cup corn or vegetable oil

1 teaspoon salt, or to taste

½ teaspoon freshly ground black pepper, or to taste

Preheat the oven to 350°. Fit a large baking pan with a metal cooling rack and arrange the bacon slices on one layer; bake until crispy, about 15–17 minutes. Cool the bacon and transfer it to a cutting board; chop it roughly and set aside.

Place the peas in a medium pot, add enough water to cover the peas by 1 inch, and set over medium-high heat. As the water simmers, skim off the foam that rises to the top; when the water comes to a boil, cover, reduce the heat to low, and simmer the peas until tender, about 40–45 minutes.

Meanwhile, fill a bowl with iced water. When the peas have finished cooking, drain and immerse them into the ice bath; let them cool for 15 minutes and then drain.

In a large bowl, combine the peas, corn, tomatoes, onions, garlic, vinegar, oil, salt, and pepper. Cover and chill for 30 minutes. Before serving, stir in the bacon and serve immediately.

Purple Hull Salad with Bacon Vinaigrette

This refreshingly sumptuous salad is the brainchild of my friend Perre Coleman Magness, who says she first got the inspiration for this recipe when she was in her car one day running errands. As she tells it, her mind was filled with images of vinaigrette flavored with bacon drippings and the crispy bacon adding a crunchy texture to summer peas. The resulting salad is colorful with contrasting textures that will surely please every food-lover's palate. I hope Perre continues to drive a lot—that is, if her culinary muse rides in the passenger seat often—because this recipe is pure genius. It's as good served as an accoutrement to grilled chicken breast as it is served as a side to a plate full of crispy fried chicken. If you can't find fresh pimiento peppers, use red bell peppers or jarred pimientos.

MAKES 8–10 SERVINGS

FOR THE SALAD
2 pounds purple hull peas
2 cups chicken broth
1 pound bacon
2 fresh pimiento peppers, cored, seeded, and finely chopped,
    or 1 (7-ounce) jar diced pimientos
4 green onions, thinly sliced (white and light green parts only)

FOR THE VINAIGRETTE
1/4 cup bacon drippings, not solidified
1/2 cup vegetable oil
4 tablespoons cider vinegar
1 tablespoon sorghum or dark honey
1 teaspoon hot sauce, or more to taste
Salt, to taste
Freshly ground black pepper, to taste

To make the salad, place the purple hulls in a large bowl and cover with water. Using your hands, gently scoop the peas out of the water (leaving any dirt and debris behind) and place them in a large pot set over medium-high heat; add the chicken broth and enough water to cover the peas by 1 inch and bring to a boil. Remove any foam that rises to the top; reduce the heat and simmer until just tender, about 30 minutes (be careful not to let them get too soft). Drain the peas in a colander and rinse them well under cold water. Transfer the peas to a large bowl and refrigerate for at least 1 hour.

Meanwhile, preheat the oven to 350°. Place the bacon strips side by side on 2 large baking sheets; cook the bacon in the oven until crispy, 15–18 minutes. Remove the bacon to paper towels to drain. Collect the drippings in a small, clean container; reserve ¼ cup for the vinaigrette (cover and chill the rest for up to 2 months or discard).

Chop the bacon coarsely; set aside. In a large bowl, toss together the peas, pimientos, and onions; set aside.

To make the vinaigrette, combine the reserved bacon drippings, oil, vinegar, sorghum, and hot sauce in a jar with a tight-fitting lid; shake vigorously to emulsify the dressing, making sure the sorghum is blended in. Season with salt and pepper.

Pour as much of the dressing as you desire over the peas, stirring to coat them well (any extra dressing should be used within a day or two). Chill the salad until ready to serve. Toss the bacon into the salad right before serving. The salad (without the bacon), covered and refrigerated, will keep for up to 2 days.

Heirloom Emily Lee Peas

I have never met anyone who is more enamored of southern peas than my good friend Fred Thompson. A well-known food writer and cookbook author, Fred is passionate about the subject of peas, and grew up eating them at his grandmother's home. Fred introduced me to the whimsical Emily Lee peas during a long conversation on heirloom peas. Emily Lees are tiny, multicolored little beads, and their color varies from one pod (or shell) to another — in one you might find peas the color of a green grasshopper, and in another they might be yellow or even black as coal. Mix them all together in one bowl and they become a vision of contrasts. Unfortunately, Emily Lees are not easy to find, but the good news is that more and more farmers are salvaging heirloom pea varieties and bringing them to market. I love them not only because they're unique but also because they're delicious. This is Fred's recipe, and as you'll see, he does the Emily Lee great justice.

MAKES 4–6 SERVINGS

---

4 cups homemade or canned, low-sodium, chicken broth
½ cup chopped onions
4 sprigs fresh thyme, tied together
3–4 × 1½-inch piece smoked or double-smoked slab bacon
3½ cups Emily Lee peas
Kosher salt and freshly ground black pepper

Bring the broth, onions, thyme, and bacon to a boil in a 3-quart saucepan over medium-high heat. Reduce heat to medium and simmer for 15 minutes.

Increase the heat to high, return the liquid to a boil, and stir in the peas. Reduce heat to medium and simmer for 30–35 minutes until the peas are tender yet a little firm. Remove from heat. Remove the thyme and discard. Remove the bacon, cut into ¼-inch slices, and stir them back into the pot. Season with salt and pepper. Serve immediately or at room temperature.

From *Fred Thompson's Southern Sides: 250 Dishes That Really Make the Plate.*
© 2012 Fred Thompson. Used by permission of the University of North Carolina Press.

Fried Bean Cakes

I couldn't think of writing a book about southern beans and peas and not include one of my favorite recipes by the late Bill Neal, founder of La Résidence and Crook's Corner restaurants in Chapel Hill. The recipe is quite easy to follow, and I like to serve it as a starter course. His combination of technique and ingredients represents a beautiful amalgamation of African and southern culinary classics. These cakes are inspired by the acarás, *or fried black-eyed pea fritters, of West African heritage but are seasoned with pork fat, beloved in the South and ever-present in a pot of peas. In fact, to get the most out of this dish, cook the peas with a piece of pork fat, preferably side meat. Neal suggests serving these with tomato sauce, but I like them served with just a splash of lemon juice.*

MAKES 2 SERVINGS

1 cup cooked and drained black-eyed peas
1 tablespoon chopped scallions
$\frac{1}{2}$–1 teaspoon chopped hot pepper
$\frac{1}{2}$ teaspoon ground cumin
Lard or bacon fat for frying

Mash the beans roughly and beat in the scallions, pepper, and cumin. Shape into 4 small patties about $\frac{2}{3}$ inch thick. Heat $\frac{1}{4}$ inch of the lard or bacon fat in a large skillet. When hot but not smoking, add the bean cakes. Fry until brown and crisp, about 4 minutes on each side. Serve hot.

From *Bill Neal's Southern Cooking*, rev. ed., by Bill Neal. © 1989 William Franklin Neal. Used by permission of the University of North Carolina Press.

Beth Weigand's Six-Week Peas

Tiny, cream-colored six-week peas are a variety of sugar crowder peas. As their name suggests, they're ready to harvest six weeks after planting and are among the first peas to make it to the summer market. Beth, a well-known food writer and southern author and a dear friend, says these peas "need a delicate hand when cooking and seasoning." For this reason, she doesn't add any seasoning meat to the pot, and finding these peas sweet enough, forgoes the pinch of sugar that many southern cooks add to their pots of field peas. Rather than combining the peas with water and bringing them to a boil, Beth boils the water first and then adds the peas because her grandmother taught her that vegetables that grow above ground must be started in boiling water and those that grow underground, like carrots and potatoes, should be cooked in cold water that is brought to a boil. I make it a point never to contradict a wise grandmother.

MAKES 4–6 SERVINGS

1–2 tablespoons extra-virgin olive oil
½ cup minced sweet onion (such as Vidalia)
2 tablespoons finely minced red bell pepper
2 pints six-week peas
6–8 sprigs fresh thyme, tied together
Salt and freshly ground black pepper, to taste

Bring 8 cups of water to a boil in a kettle. Heat the olive oil in a medium pot over medium heat. Add the onions and the bell pepper; cook, stirring, until they begin to become tender and translucent. Add the peas, thyme, and enough boiling water to cover the peas by 1 inch. Return the water to a soft boil; reduce the heat to low and simmer gently until the peas are tender, 15–20 minutes, skimming off any foam that rises to the top.

When the peas are tender, remove the thyme; drain the peas and transfer to a platter; season with salt and pepper and serve.

Beth Weigand's Six-Week Peas and Tomato Salad

In the South, tomatoes and peas grow side by side in the summertime. Since they share the spotlight during the same season, it's not surprising that they also marry perfectly on the plate. Just in case you have any leftovers in a pot of six week peas, Beth suggests making this easy side salad. The dressing is simply shaken in a jar and poured over the peas.

MAKES 4 SERVINGS

2–3 cups Beth Weigand's Six-Week Peas (page 47),
    at room temperature
1 tablespoon white wine vinegar
½ teaspoon Dijon mustard
½ teaspoon salt
Several grinds of black pepper
⅓ cup extra-virgin olive oil
Several lettuce leaves (your favorite kind)
2 large ripe tomatoes, sliced thickly
Basil leaves, to taste

Place the peas in a medium bowl. In a small jar with a lid, place the vinegar, mustard, salt, and pepper; shake to mix the ingredients together. Add the olive oil and shake vigorously to emulsify. Pour the dressing over the peas and stir.

Place a layer of lettuce leaves on four small plates and layer several slices of tomatoes on each. Spoon the peas over the tomatoes and decorate with basil leaves.

Dixie Lees with Ham

These small, brown peas, frequently served on barbecue platters where I live, pack a lot of flavor. They may be among the smallest field peas, but Dixie Lees produce a dark, rich pot likker. I simply adore them and marvel at how just a few ingredients mixed together in a pot can result in such a deeply flavored delicacy. Dixie Lees grow in slim, green pods that are about 7 inches long. Every summer, I find them at my favorite roadside stand in the Sandhills, already shelled and dried, and packed in little plastic bags that weigh exactly one pound. I make sure to purchase plenty—enough to last me until the following year. You could embellish the likker with anything you like, such as a handful of chopped tomatoes or a spicy chile—but I prefer the simple taste of smoked ham and peas. These generally don't need to be salted as the ham is salty enough. I particularly love these ladled over white or brown rice.

MAKES 8 SERVINGS

---

1 (12-ounce) ham hock
1 pound dried Dixie Lee peas (about 2½ cups),
    cleaned of debris
½ cup finely chopped white or spring onions

Place the ham hock in a 3-quart pot and cover with 6 cups of water. Bring to a boil over medium-high heat; cover, reduce the heat to low, and simmer for 40 minutes.

Add the peas and onions and bring the liquid back to a boil; cover, reduce the heat to low and simmer until the peas are soft and tender, 1½–2 hours (see Note). Remove the peas from the heat. Remove the ham hock and pull it apart into bite-size pieces; return the ham to the pot and discard the bone. Serve immediately.

NOTE ❋ The older the peas, the longer they will take to cook.

Succotash

This archetypal mélange of corn and lima beans is believed to be one of the oldest recipes in the United States, and it still remains a favorite of southern cooks. It originated with Native Americans and was likely made with butter beans. It would not have been seasoned with pork since pork was introduced by the Spaniards years later. The word "succotash" derives from the Narragansett Indian word sukquttahash, *which means "boiled whole ear of corn." During the summer months when fresh corn and butter beans are abundant, this dish makes a frequent appearance on my table. In winter, I use frozen corn and my stash of frozen beans from summer. For a vegetarian option, omit the bacon and use olive oil instead. This is a terrific side dish for fat, juicy grilled pork chops.*

MAKES 8 SERVINGS

5–6 slices smoked bacon (about 5 ounces), coarsely chopped

1½ cups chopped Vidalia onion

1½ cups chopped red bell pepper

2 large garlic cloves, minced

4 cups corn kernels (about 5 large ears)

3 cups cooked butter beans or baby lima beans

1½ cups seeded and chopped zucchini

1 teaspoon ground sage

1 teaspoon salt

¼ teaspoon freshly ground black pepper

Place the bacon in a 12-inch skillet set over medium-high heat and cook, stirring, until it has rendered its fat and is just beginning to crisp, about 4 minutes. Add the onion and bell pepper, and cook, stirring, until the onion begins to soften, about 4 minutes. Add the garlic and cook for about 30 seconds or until fragrant. Add the corn, butter beans or lima beans, zucchini, sage, salt, and pepper and continue cooking until the zucchini begins to soften but remains a vibrant green color, about 4–5 minutes. Serve immediately.

Butter Bean, Corn, and Tomato Salad

Most southern salads are simple to make, and this one showcases the flavors of summer. It offers a perfect trifecta of flavors (sweet, nutty, and slightly acidic), colors (red, yellow, and green), and textures (creamy, crunchy, and soft). Every time I make it, I wonder how such an easy recipe can yield such a delicious dish. Try it, and you'll see what I mean. If you let this salad rest for an hour or so before serving, the tomatoes will release their juices and add to the flavor of the dressing. Use fresh corn, scraped directly from the cobs, and fresh beans, if you can.

MAKES 4–6 SERVINGS

2 cups butter beans (about ½ pound)

2 cups corn kernels

2 cups seeded, chopped plum tomatoes

2 tablespoons apple cider vinegar, or to taste

1 teaspoon salt, or to taste

¼ teaspoon freshly ground black pepper

¼ cup corn or vegetable oil

Place the beans in a pot and cover with water by 2 inches. Bring to a boil and cook for 5 minutes, skimming off the foam that rises to the top; cover, reduce the heat, and simmer for 35–40 minutes or until tender.

Meanwhile, fill a bowl with iced water. When the beans have finished cooking, drain and immerse them in the ice bath until cool. Drain the peas and transfer them to a large bowl; add the corn and tomatoes.

In a small bowl, whisk together the vinegar, salt, and pepper. Whisk in the oil and pour the dressing over the salad; stir until combined.

Butter Beans with Butter and Parsley

When butter beans make their appearance at farmers' markets, they announce the arrival of pea season in the South, but the season for them doesn't last long. Like many, I trek to the Raleigh Farmers' Market at the start of every summer and buy them already shelled in bulk. My husband is sometimes an accidental recruit in my kitchen, and I often request his help when I'm blanching butter beans in bulk—sometimes ten pounds at a time—so that I can freeze them and have them on hand for months to come. He knows that in the end, the recompense will be delicious, and since he loves these green goddesses as much as I do, he kindly acquiesces. Since butter beans need little to enhance their sweet, nutty flavor, I usually use this recipe to prepare our first batch of peas every year. During the summer, I also like to stir in a couple of tablespoons of thinly sliced basil, which adds a touch of sweetness to these already succulent beans. If you don't have access to fresh butter beans, avoid the canned variety and buy frozen.

MAKES 4–6 SERVINGS

1 pound fresh butter beans
4–6 cups water
2 tablespoons unsalted butter
$\frac{1}{2}$ teaspoon salt
$\frac{1}{4}$ cup finely chopped flat-leaf parsley

Place the butter beans in a medium pot, add the water, and bring to a boil over medium-high heat. Cover, reduce the heat, and simmer for 15–20 minutes or until tender. Drain the beans and transfer to a bowl; stir in the butter, salt, and parsley. Serve at once.

Mess of Peas

My southern friends tell me that a mess of peas is just the right amount needed to feed the right number of people at your table. This recipe calls for fresh or frozen peas, but you can also use dried peas; keep in mind, though they'll need about an hour (or longer, if they're old) to cook thoroughly. I generally don't add any salt to this dish because the ham provides enough seasoning. Serve this with freshly baked cornbread and a batch of fried green tomatoes. Making a mess in the kitchen never tasted this good before!

MAKES 4 SERVINGS

½ pound smoked country ham
1 pound fresh or frozen field peas (any kind)
1 jalapeño pepper
2 teaspoons sugar
½ teaspoon freshly ground black pepper
Salt, to taste

Place the ham in a medium stockpot, cover with water (about 6 cups), and bring to a boil over medium-high heat; cover, reduce the heat to low, and simmer for 30 minutes. Stir in the peas, jalapeño, sugar, and pepper. Cover and simmer for 30–40 minutes more or until the peas are soft (but not mushy). Remove the jalapeño and discard. Remove the ham with tongs and transfer it to a cutting board; chop it into bite-size pieces and return to the pot. Season with salt. Serve the peas with or without the pot likker.

HOW TO FREEZE SOUTHERN PEAS

First, rinse the peas well in cold water to remove any dirt or debris. Bring a large pot of water to a rolling boil. Fill a large bowl with cold water and a generous amount of ice. Add the peas to the boiling water; cook for 2 minutes and with a sieve or a small strainer immediately transfer them to the iced water to stop the cooking process. Once cool, drain them well. Dry the peas between kitchen towels and divide them into small freezer-safe bags; freeze them for up to 6 months. There is no need to thaw peas before cooking them.

HOW TO COOK SOUTHERN PEAS

Fresh peas must be cooked before being used in most recipes, such as succotash and salads. To do this, place the peas in a pot and cover them by 2 inches of water. Bring the water to a boil; cover, reduce the heat, and simmer the peas for 35–40 minutes or until fork-tender. If the peas are previously frozen, cook an additional 5–10 minutes, or until they're tender.

Pole Beans with Potatoes and Double-Smoked Bacon

Pole beans are available from July to October. These green beans grow tall, climbing on poles that keep the vines from collapsing with the weight of the pods—thus their name. They take longer to cook than bush beans and produce a light, scrumptious pot likker. Most of them, like the Kentucky Wonder, have strings that must be removed before cooking. To do this, snap off one end of the bean and pull off the string on one side; turn the bean over, snap the other end, and pull off the string on the other. Double-smoked bacon is easy to find in the South, but you can use any other kind of bacon. For this recipe, I, like most southern cooks, prefer my bacon cut into cubes; this helps it retain a meaty consistency when its cooked. Green beans and new potatoes are harvested at the same time in the South and just as often are cooked together. If you're among those who are accustomed to preparing stringless green beans, which are generally cooked only briefly and eaten crispy, and shy away from the long-cooked, southern-style ones, try this recipe. You'll understand why sometimes green beans just taste better when they've been allowed to bubble leisurely in a pot.

MAKES 4–6 SERVINGS

---

4 ounces double-smoked bacon (or smoked bacon slab),
   cut into tiny cubes

1 pound pole beans (such as Kentucky Wonders),
   cut into thirds

4 cups water

1 pound new potatoes (red or white), quartered

1 teaspoon salt

¼ teaspoon freshly ground black pepper

Set a 3- to 4-quart pot over medium-high heat. Add the bacon and cook until it has rendered most of its fat but is still soft (do not let it crisp), about 1½–2 minutes. Add the beans and the water. Increase the heat to high and bring the water to a boil, scraping up the brown bits at the bottom of the pan. Cover, reduce the heat to low, and simmer for 20 minutes. Add the potatoes, salt, and pepper; increase the heat to medium-high and bring the liquid back to a boil. Cover, reduce the heat, and simmer until the potatoes are fork-tender, about 20–25 minutes. Serve in deep bowls with some of the pot likker.

Half Runners with Seasoning

Half runner beans are long, semiflat, light-green beans that appear on a tangle of low-growing vines that resembles a bush. Heirloom green beans like half runners are meant to be cooked long and slow. Southerners are often accused of overcooking vegetables, but there is a reason they do. Half runners, for example, become more succulent the longer they cook. Before you cook them, you must remove the feathery but sturdy strings that run along either side of them. To do this, simply snap one end of the bean and pull off the string along one side; turn the bean over, snap the other end and pull off the string along the other side. When they're cooking, they'll split down the middle so some of the tiny white beans inside will be released into the pot likker. In the South, the piece of pork added to the pot is known as seasoning, and that's all these beans need to garner their best flavor.

MAKES 6–8 SERVINGS

1 pound half runners, washed and strings removed

8 cups water

8 ounces country cured ham (preferably center cut and
   end parts)

1 teaspoon salt, or to taste

Place the beans in a 6- to 8-quart Dutch oven set over medium-high heat; add the water, ham, and salt and bring to a boil. Cover, reduce the heat to low, and simmer for 45 minutes to 1 hour.

Remove the ham and chop it into bite-size pieces; return to the pot. Serve the beans in bowls with some of the liquid.

New Southern Dishes

What we think of today as the Global South, with its wonderful convergence of people from all over the world on the American South, has inspired a culinary movement in which ingredients, flavors, and cooking techniques from many different countries and cultures grace the southern table. It is impossible to eat in the South today and not encounter Latino, Vietnamese, Greek, Jewish, Caribbean, and other cultural imprints in the modern flavors that meld at the table seamlessly with southern food. From the "red-hot" tamales of the Mississippi Delta to Louisiana's Cajun Vietnamese crawfish boiled with lemongrass and hot sauce, Global Southern cuisine is vibrant and effervescently evolving. Beans and peas lend themselves perfectly to these new interpretations that marry the classic southern culinary flavors with those from around the world.
In this chapter, you'll find some of the dishes born from this movement—some created by highly esteemed chefs and others by innovative cooks in their own kitchens. One thing is true: no matter the many flavors that come together in these bean and pea recipes, they all stay true to their southern roots.

Mean Bean Burgers with Chipotle Mayo

I am a meat lover, but, given a choice, I'd eat these bean burgers over a beef burger any day! They're perfectly seasoned with spices and their texture is just right—not too hard or too mushy—and holds up to all of my favorite toppings. There are a few things to keep in mind when creating the perfect bean burgers: First, they need to chill for a while before you cook them or they'll fall apart. Second, they must be dredged in flour before they hit the oil in the pan to ensure that they form a golden crust. Finally, they must spend a bit of time in the oven after they've been seared in the oil so that they can cook through without burning; baking also helps them retain their shape. I prefer to cook my own beans for these burgers (see page 94), because canned beans can be too mushy. If you do use canned beans, gradually add more breadcrumbs until the mixture holds together.

MAKES 6–7 SERVINGS

FOR THE CHIPOTLE MAYO

1 cup mayonnaise

1 medium canned chipotle chile in adobo, finely minced

2 teaspoons adobo sauce from the canned chipotles

FOR THE BURGERS

1 cup chopped white onion

3 garlic cloves, chopped

4 cups cooked black beans, drained well, divided

1/2 cup chopped cilantro (leaves and tender stems)

1/2 cup bread crumbs

1 egg

1 teaspoon salt

1 teaspoon ground cumin

1/2 teaspoon ground coriander

1/2 teaspoon ancho chile powder

¼ teaspoon freshly ground black pepper
¼ cup all-purpose flour (for dredging)
⅓–½ cup extra-virgin olive oil
6–7 kaiser or hamburger rolls, split lengthwise
6–7 Bibb lettuce leaves
1 large tomato, thinly sliced
Ketchup, to taste (optional)

To make the chipotle mayo, in a small bowl combine the mayonnaise, chipotle, and adobo sauce; stir to combine. Cover with plastic wrap and chill until ready to use (up to 4 days).

To make the burgers, line a large baking pan with parchment paper; set aside. Place the onion and garlic in the bowl of a food processor fitted with the metal blade; pulse 3 times at 5-second intervals or until finely chopped (stopping to scrape down the sides of the bowl as needed).

Add 3 cups of the beans and the cilantro, bread crumbs, egg, salt, cumin, coriander, chile powder, and pepper and pulse 6–8 times at 5-second intervals until the mixture is smooth (stopping to scrape down the sides of the bowl as needed). Transfer the mixture to a medium bowl; stir in the remaining beans until well distributed.

Using a heaping ½ cup of the mixture each, form 3½ × ½-inch patties and place them on the prepared pan. Chill the patties for at least 30 minutes (up to 2 hours).

Preheat the oven to 375°. Spray a large baking sheet with cooking spray (or oil lightly) and set aside.

Place the flour in a shallow baking pan and dredge the patties in the flour, removing any excess flour by patting them between your hands. Heat half of the oil in a 10-inch nonstick skillet set over medium-high heat and, working in batches (and adding the remaining oil as needed), cook the patties on both sides until golden, about 1½–2 minutes per side (see Note); set them on the prepared sheet.

Bake for 15–20 minutes. Brush the rolls with the chipotle mayonnaise; dress with lettuce and tomato. Place a bean patty inside each roll and top with ketchup, if using.

NOTE ✳ If the burgers are browning too quickly in the pan, reduce the heat to medium. It's important to cook them just until they form a golden-brown crust; baking them will cook them through.

Black Bean "Sombreros" with Avocado Crema

Once fried, these crispy little appetizers resemble sombreros. They're creamy inside and have just enough heat to make the palate tingle. I make these in large quantities—the recipe easily doubles and triples or quadruples—because they can be frozen after they're assembled and go directly from freezer to fryer. I serve these with a vibrantly flavored avocado crema, store-bought salsa, and sour cream. They're fun, very original, and absolutely adorable. Use canned refried beans, but be sure to process them to remove any lumps or they'll cause the wontons to tear (my favorite brand is Ducal by GOYA, because they're already smooth).

MAKES 4–6 SERVINGS

FOR THE AVOCADO CREMA

1 Hass avocado

1 cup sour cream

2 tablespoons lime juice, or to taste

¾ teaspoon salt, or to taste

¼ teaspoon freshly ground black pepper, or to taste

FOR THE "SOMBREROS"

1 (12-ounce, 50-piece) package square wonton wrappers

¾ cup canned refried black beans

2 small jalapeño peppers, cut into paper-thin rounds (seeded and deveined for less heat)

Paste made with ¼ cup water plus 4 tablespoons all-purpose flour

Vegetable or peanut oil for frying

To make the avocado crema, combine the avocado, sour cream, lime juice, salt, and pepper in a medium bowl; using a fork or a small potato masher, mash it all well together until smooth. Cover with plastic wrap and chill it until ready to serve (you may prepare the crema one day ahead).

To make the sombreros, fit a large baking pan with a metal cooling rack and line two baking pans with parchment paper; set aside.

Spread out the wonton wrappers on a clean surface, keeping them covered with a clean towel as you work so that they don't dry out. Working with two wonton wrappers at a time, place 1 teaspoon of the beans in the center of one and top with a few pieces of jalapeño. Using your index finger, apply some of the paste to the edges of the second wonton and place it on top of the wonton with the beans. Seal the wontons, making sure to press out any air bubbles as you do so (so the wontons don't burst when cooked). Repeat until all of the wontons are filled (you should have 24–25 pieces), keeping them covered as you work.

Using a 2½-inch round cookie cutter (with fluted edges, if possible), cut the filled wontons into rounds and place them on the prepared baking pans. Place them in the refrigerator for 20–30 minutes, keeping them covered with the towel (see Note).

In a large skillet with high sides, heat 2 inches of oil to 360° (or use a deep fryer according to the manufacturer's directions); working in batches and using your hands, gently place the filled wontons in the oil. Fry them until golden, about 45 seconds to 1 minute, turning them over halfway through. Using a slotted spoon, transfer them to the prepared rack to drain. Serve immediately with the crema.

NOTE ❀ For best results, cook these soon after assembling them, or you can freeze them for up to 2 months. Freeze them in single layer; once solid, transfer to freezer-safe bags. Don't thaw them before frying; add 10–15 extra seconds to the frying time.

White Bean Salad with Raisins and Ginger

Sweet, zesty vinaigrette adds a level of sumptuousness to humble white beans in this salad that is sure to blow your mind and surprise your palate. As unusual as it may appear, many cultures combine beans with sweet and sour sauces. You'll even find sweetened beans cooked with chocolate in Central American desserts, and beans used to make delicate sweets in Asia. Here in the South, baked bean dishes enhanced with molasses or sorghum are quite common, and they're often served alongside barbecue. I've transformed this idea into a salad that's as elegant as it is exotic. You'll have to trust me on this one: raisins and beans go very well together in this salad. Serve it as a bed for poached or grilled salmon.

MAKES 6–8 SERVINGS

½ cup white wine vinegar

¼ cup balsamic vinegar

⅓ cup golden raisins

1 (2-inch) piece fresh ginger, peeled and sliced in quarters

2 teaspoons finely chopped tarragon (optional)

¼ cup unsulfured molasses

2 teaspoons salt, or to taste

½ teaspoon freshly ground black pepper, or to taste

¾ cup extra-virgin olive oil

1 pound great northern white beans, cooked, rinsed,
   and drained

2 large garlic cloves, minced

2 cups seeded and finely chopped plum tomatoes
   (about 4–5 large)

1 (7-ounce) jar diced pimientos, drained

⅓ cup minced shallots

¼ cup minced leeks (white and light green parts only)

¾ cup finely chopped Italian parsley

Combine the vinegars and raisins in a small, nonreactive saucepan set over medium heat. Bring the mixture to a simmer and cook for 2–3 minutes. Remove the raisins with a slotted spoon and set them aside in a small bowl. Stir the ginger and tarragon (if using) into the vinegar. Bring the mixture to a simmer again over medium heat and cook for 1 minute; turn off the heat and let the vinegar mixture cool completely, about 20 minutes.

When the vinegar is cool to the touch, strain it into a medium bowl; discard the ginger and the tarragon. Add the molasses and stir until completely dissolved; add the salt and pepper. Slowly whisk in the olive oil and set aside.

In a large bowl, combine the beans, garlic, tomatoes, pimientos, shallots, leeks, and parsley. Pour the vinaigrette over the salad and stir well; add the reserved raisins and stir again. Chill the salad for at least 2 hours (and up to 24) before serving.

Simmered Black-Eyed Peas
with Tomatoes

Summertime in the South spells an abundance of peas and to-matoes and, not surprisingly, what grows at the same time also cooks together well. I came across this rich and comforting dish in the extraordinary book Matzoh Ball Gumbo: Culinary Tales of the Jewish South, *written by my friend Marcie Cohen-Ferris. Marcie, who is a food historian and author, got this recipe from Miriam Cohen, a member of the Congregation Or VeShalom in Atlanta, where the Sephardic community holds a food festival every December. Marcie says that this dish is traditionally served with a Sephardic rice-and-tomato dish called pink rice, which is reminiscent of the red rice eaten in the Low Country (Marcie's son calls it "Jewish soul food"). Here is an example of how Jewish and southern culinary traditions are threaded together to form a won-derful tapestry of flavors that celebrates both cultures.*

MAKES 6–8 SIDE-DISH SERVINGS

2 tablespoons olive oil

1 large onion, chopped

2 garlic cloves, minced

1 medium tomato, chopped

½ teaspoon thyme

¾ teaspoon kosher salt

½ teaspoon freshly ground black pepper

2 boxes (10 ounces each) frozen black-eyed peas or
fresh black-eyed peas (add more water if necessary)

1½ cups water (or more if using fresh peas)

In a large, heavy saucepan, heat the oil over medium heat. Add the onion and garlic and cook, stirring often, until tender, about 4 minutes. Add the tomato, thyme, salt, and pepper and cook, stirring often, until the tomato starts to soften, about 2 minutes. Stir in the black-eyed peas and water; bring to a boil. Reduce the heat to low, cover and simmer until the peas are tender, about 30 minutes. Taste and correct the seasoning, if necessary. Serve the peas hot or warm.

From *Matzoh Ball Gumbo: Culinary Tales of the Jewish South*, by Marcie Cohen Ferris. © 2005 Marcie Cohen Ferris. Used by permission of the University of North Carolina Press.

Fried Green Tomato Stacks with Pea Salsa and Imitation Crabmeat

I was inspired to make this New Southern–Latino twist on a dish made with crabmeat that I first tried at e2 emeril's eatery, Emeril Lagasse's restaurant in Charlotte, North Carolina. Here, crispy, fried green tomatoes sit atop a bed of pea salsa, and between the layers of tomatoes hides a sweet remoulade made with imitation crabmeat. I love this kind of crabmeat in this recipe because its sweet flavor interplays seamlessly with those of the other ingredients. The imitation crab is made with pollock, a fish that has been shaped and cured to resemble crab or lobster meat—because the poor thing is so ugly that we wouldn't eat it otherwise—but you can use shrimp, crabmeat, or lobster if you prefer. Each bite features a touch of acidity and a kiss of sweetness, creating an irresistible agro dolce *(or sweet-and-sour) combo that works each and every time. It's refreshing, visually stunning, and absolutely succulent.*

MAKES 4 SERVINGS

FOR THE SALSA
1 pound crowder peas or black-eyed peas, cooked, drained, and chilled
¼ cup finely chopped Vidalia onion
2 tablespoons finely chopped red bell pepper
2 tablespoons finely chopped flat-leaf parsley (leaves and tender stems)
¼ cup fresh lemon juice
¼ cup extra-virgin olive oil
1 teaspoon stone-ground mustard
¼ teaspoon ground cumin
½ teaspoon salt, or to taste
¼ teaspoon freshly ground black pepper

FOR THE CRAB
6 ounces imitation crabmeat, shredded
2 tablespoons mayonnaise

1 large egg, lightly beaten
½ cup buttermilk
¼ cup all-purpose flour
½ cup finely ground yellow cornmeal
2 large green tomatoes, cut into eight ½-inch-thick slices
Vegetable oil for frying

To make the salsa, in a medium bowl, combine the peas, onions, bell pepper, parsley, lemon juice, oil, mustard, cumin, salt, and pepper; set aside.

In a small bowl, combine the crab and the mayonnaise; set aside. Line a baking pan with parchment paper; set aside.

To prepare the tomatoes, in a shallow bowl, combine the egg and buttermilk. Place the flour and cornmeal in 2 separate shallow dishes. Working with one slice at a time, dredge the tomatoes in the flour, dip in the egg mixture to coat on both sides, and coat each side with the cornmeal. Place the tomatoes in the parchment-lined baking pan.

Fit a large baking pan with a metal cooling rack. In a large skillet with high sides heat ½ inch of oil to 360° (or use a deep fryer according to the manufacturer's directions); working in two batches, using your fingers, carefully, place the tomato slices in the oil. Fry them on both sides until golden, about 2 minutes per side (use two forks to help turn them over). Using the two forks or a slotted spoon, transfer to the prepared rack to drain.

To plate, place ¼ of the pea salsa onto four plates, making a bed for the tomatoes. Place a slice of fried tomato on top of the salsa and top with an eighth of the crab mixture; top with a second slice of tomato and top with another eighth of the crab. Serve immediately.

NOTE ❋ Keep the crab and peas in the refrigerator until ready to use; they may be prepared up to 1 day ahead of time. The tomatoes must be fried shortly after they're coated with cornmeal and should be consumed immediately after frying.

Yellow-Eyed Peas with Tasso and Sofrito

My friend and colleague Elizabeth Wiegand introduced me to yellow-eyed peas. These peas are similar to black-eyed peas, but their white bodies are dressed with a golden eye of a mustardlike hue that makes them look exotic. They're sold at the many roadside farmers' stands that carry peas in North Carolina during the summer. I usually buy mine dried by the bucketful at a stand on Highway 211 in the Sandhills—it's hard to resist when they are so pretty to look at and so delicious to eat. You can order them online from many sources. Tasso is the specialty smoked pork butt (shoulder) of Louisiana, and it's the perfect partner for peas and beans. Here, it provides the peas with plenty of meaty and smoky flavor. Sofrito is a Latin American flavor base made with onions and bell peppers. I serve this New Southern–Latino rendition over a mound of fluffy white rice, with a side of collard greens and accompanied by a good medium-bodied red wine.

MAKES 6–8 SERVINGS

1 pound yellow-eyed peas, soaked overnight

¾ pound tasso or smoked ham hock

1 bay leaf

2 tablespoons extra-virgin olive oil

1 cup finely chopped yellow onion

2 large garlic cloves, minced

1 cup diced tomatoes (may use canned)

1 (7-ounce) jar diced pimientos, drained

½ teaspoon thyme

1½ teaspoons salt, or more to taste (depending on how salty the ham is)

½ teaspoon freshly ground black pepper

2 tablespoons chopped flat-leaf parsley

Place the peas, tasso, and bay leaf in a 5- to 6-quart pot set over medium-high heat and cover with cold water by 2 inches. Bring to a boil; cover, reduce the heat to low, and simmer for 60–75 minutes or until the peas are fork-tender. Remove the bay leaf and discard. Remove the tasso and set aside until cool enough to handle.

Heat the oil in a 10-inch skillet over medium-high heat. Add the onion and cook until softened, about 3–4 minutes. Add the garlic and cook until fragrant, about 20 seconds. Add the tomatoes, pimientos, thyme, salt, and pepper, and continue cooking until thickened or about 3 minutes. Shred or chop the tasso.

Add the cooked vegetables to the pot of peas and bring to a simmer over medium heat. Add the tasso. Increase the heat to medium-high and bring to a boil; reduce the heat to medium and simmer for 15 minutes or until the liquid has reduced slightly. Stir in the parsley; taste and add more salt if needed, and serve.

Purple Hull and
Benne Seed Hummus

This creamy, sultry dip has just the right balance of tanginess and spice to please most palates. Hummus is a Middle Eastern spread that has become very trendy in the past decade, and it's usually made with chickpeas, but purple hulls lend themselves perfectly to this unconventional treatment because they cook to a velvety consistency that makes them easy to purée. Tahini is sesame paste, with a consistency similar to peanut butter and you can find it in most grocery stores. Benne *is the African word for sesame seeds, and they were introduced into the South during the African diaspora, when they were used in candies, cakes, bread, soups, and stews. Make this recipe whenever you find yourself with an abundance of peas during the summer months. It makes a great dip for crudités, and it's also perfect substitute for mayonnaise on sandwiches. Serve it with toasted pita bread, chips, or crackers.*

MAKES 6 SERVINGS

3 large garlic cloves, chopped
1 pound cooked purple hull peas, drained
⅓ cup sesame seed paste (tahini)
¼ cup fresh lemon juice, or to taste
1 teaspoon salt, or to taste
¼ teaspoon freshly ground black pepper, or to taste
1 tablespoon extra-virgin olive oil
Pinch cayenne pepper (optional)

In a food processor fitted with a metal blade, pulse the garlic for three (5-second) intervals. Add the purple hulls and tahini; pulse until smooth, about 10–12 (5-second) intervals, stopping to scrape down the sides of the bowl, if needed. Add the lemon juice, salt, and pepper and process until combined. Transfer the mixture to a medium bowl; drizzle with the olive oil and sprinkle with cayenne pepper (if using).

NOTE ❋ This dip will keep in the refrigerator, if well covered, for up to 5 days.

Speckled Butter Bean Ceviche with Grilled Shrimp

Nutty beans meet vibrant citrus and spicy chiles. Then they're topped with sweet, plump shrimp, yielding a salad that features the colors of autumn. Speckled butter beans are among the most beautiful members of the lima bean family (Phaseolus lunatus). When dried, they are a purplish-brown color, mottled with pinkish spots. When cooked, they produce a dark pot likker, and although they lose their speckled appearance, they retain their beautiful color. It's not as crazy to call this salad a ceviche as you may first think. The beans are cured in the same citrus and chile dressing used in traditional Peruvian ceviches, and in Latin America this qualifies as one. Ají amarillo peppers are found pickled, in jars or cans, in most Latin American stores. If you can't find them, use fresh jalapeños instead. Shrimp are measured by how many are in one pound and the ideal shrimp for this recipe are large and plump. Not all shrimp turn pink when cooked (it depends on the variety); make sure you cook them well but take them off the grill when they begin to curl (a sign of doneness). For a vegetarian option, simply omit the shrimp.

MAKES 4 SERVINGS

FOR THE CEVICHE

1/2 pound speckled butter beans, cooked, drained, and chilled

1/2 cup fresh lemon juice

1/2 cup chopped Vidalia onion

1/4 cup chopped cilantro (leaves and tender stems)

3 ají amarillo peppers, peeled, seeded, deveined, and chopped

1 teaspoon salt, or to taste

1/4 teaspoon freshly ground black pepper, or to taste

24 shrimp (16–21 count)
¼ teaspoon garlic powder
¼ teaspoon ground cumin
¼ teaspoon salt
¼ teaspoon freshly ground black pepper
4 large metal or bamboo skewers

To make the ceviche, in a medium bowl, combine the beans, lemon juice, onion, cilantro, ajíes, salt, and pepper; mix well and chill for at least 2 hours (up to overnight), stirring occasionally.

To prepare the shrimp, peel and devein them, leaving the tails intact. Place 6 shrimp on each skewer. In a small bowl, combine the garlic powder, cumin, salt, and pepper; sprinkle the mixture over the shrimp, making sure to coat them well. Heat an outdoor grill or indoor grill pan until very hot. Grill the shrimp for 3 minutes on the first side or until they've turned opaque; turn and grill for 3–4 more minutes or until cooked through. Transfer the bean ceviche to a large platter and top with the shrimp skewers.

Green Bean, White Lima Bean, and Andouille Ragout with Rice

This recipe reminds me of lazy days dining in the French Quarter of New Orleans, where French, Creole, and Cajun flavors embrace each other in dishes filled with spices. In this dish, each bite offers a hint of sweetness hidden among the bold flavors that pleasantly surprises the palate. Spicy, creamy, hearty, and buttery, beans prepared this way are the perfect topping for fluffy rice, and perhaps that's why they're often served this way. Lima beans are so maligned, and it's too bad because they can truly be some of the most delectable legumes you will ever eat. I love their velvety texture, the way they melt in the mouth, and how they absorb seasonings as they cook. This recipe is an excellent dish for entertaining, so luxurious and elegant that you will be proud to serve it to your most esteemed guests.

MAKES 4–6 SERVINGS

1 pound dried white lima beans, cleaned of debris

¼ cup extra-virgin olive oil

2 cups chopped Vidalia onion

1½ cups chopped red bell pepper

6 large garlic cloves, thinly sliced

12 sprigs fresh thyme or 1 teaspoon dried

12 ounces andouille sausage (or Spanish chorizo),
cut into bite-size pieces

½ pound green beans (such as Blue Lakes), trimmed and
cut crosswise into thirds

½ cup chicken broth or water

1½ teaspoons salt, or to taste

¼ teaspoon freshly ground black pepper, or to taste

3 tablespoons unsalted butter

4–6 cups cooked long-grain white rice

Place the lima beans in a large bowl and cover them with cold water; soak overnight (or at least 6 hours).

Drain and rinse the lima beans and place them in a 6- to 8-quart pot. Add enough cold water to cover the beans by 3 inches and bring to a boil over medium-high heat, skimming off the foam that rises to the top. Reduce the heat to medium and continue simmering the beans (replenishing the water with more boiling water, as needed, to keep them covered by 3 inches) for 45–60 minutes or until fork-tender. Drain and rinse the beans under cold running water and set aside.

In a 12-inch skillet with high sides (or in a large pot), heat the oil over medium-high heat. Add the onion and bell pepper, cooking until softened, about 3–4 minutes. Add the garlic and thyme, and cook for 20 seconds or until fragrant. Add the sausage and cook, stirring constantly, for 3–4 minutes or until the sausage begins to turn golden and has rendered its fat. Add the green beans and cook for 1 minute to set the color. Add the lima beans and broth and bring to a boil, making sure to scrape the bottom of the pan well to deglaze the pan. Add the salt and pepper; cover, reduce the heat to low, and cook for 15 minutes. If using fresh thyme, remove the sprigs now, and adjust the seasonings to your liking. Right before serving, stir in the butter, just until melted. Serve in bowls over the rice.

Smoky New Potato, Green Bean, and Bacon Salad

This smoky and savory salad is a great side dish to serve with barbecue. The creamy and lemony dressing coats every single ingredient, making each bite as delicious as the last. Green beans, potatoes, and bacon often go hand in hand in southern cuisine, and most often, you'll find them served steaming hot from the pot. I adore potato salads in all their guises, so I came up with a way of combining the same elements and transforming them into this cold dish. Let's face it, everything tastes better with bacon, and this salad is no exception. In order to enhance the smokiness of the bacon, I incorporate another favorite ingredient of mine, one that has become quite trendy in the last few years: smoked Spanish paprika. Also known as pimentón, *it's often paired with potatoes. I recommend adding the bacon just before you serve this salad so that it retains its crunch.*

MAKES 8–10 SERVINGS

2½ pounds new potatoes

1 pound green beans (such as Blue Lakes), trimmed

1 cup mayonnaise

Zest of 2 lemons

¼ cup fresh lemon juice, or to taste

¼ cup sour cream

2 teaspoons salt, or to taste

1 teaspoon sweet, smoked Spanish paprika

¼ teaspoon freshly ground black pepper, or to taste

1 pound thick-cut bacon slices

¼ cup minced chives

Place the potatoes in a 6- to 8-quart pot or Dutch oven. Add enough cold water to cover the potatoes by 2–3 inches and bring to a boil over medium-high heat. Cook until the potatoes are fork-tender, about 20–22 minutes, reducing the heat to medium if the water is boiling over. Remove the potatoes with a slotted spoon and set them in a bowl to cool for about 30 minutes, leaving the water in the pot and adding more water to fill it again.

Fill a large bowl with iced water. Bring the pot of water to a rolling boil and add the green beans; boil until tender, about 6 minutes. Drain and immediately plunge them into the iced water to stop the cooking; cool completely, drain again, and set aside.

Peel the potatoes, cut them into bite-size pieces, and place them in a large bowl. Cut the green beans crosswise into thirds and add them to the potatoes.

In a medium bowl, whisk together the mayonnaise, lemon zest, lemon juice, sour cream, salt, paprika, and pepper. Add the dressing to the vegetables and toss well to coat; cover with plastic wrap and chill for at least 30 minutes or up to 2 days.

About 30 minutes before serving, preheat the oven to 350° and line a large baking pan with parchment paper.

Place the bacon slices side by side on the pan and bake for 15–18 minutes or until crispy. Transfer the bacon to a plate lined with paper towels to drain off the fat; when cool, chop it coarsely. Adjust the seasonings in the salad, if needed. Stir in the bacon and the chives.

NOTE ❋ Cold food tastes blander to our palate than hot food, so always taste cold food before serving, as it will often need to be slightly reseasoned.

Jill Warren Lucas's Dilly Beans

My friend Jill Warren Lucas is a fabulous writer and cook. One of her fields of expertise is canning, so I asked her to develop a special recipe for this book and she kindly created this great rendition of a southern favorite. Jill says that it's best to make these zingy pickled green beans during the summer, when they are at their brightest green and very crisp; it's also the time of year when they're inexpensive and widely available at local farmers' markets. She warns that unless the best beans are used, these won't retain their beautiful or "magical snap." Canning salt can be found in grocery stores and shops that carry canning supplies. Do not substitute any other type of salt. Jill says that the longer you wait to eat these beans, the tastier they'll be. These are addictive, and in my house, they don't last long.

MAKES 4 PINTS

2 pounds green beans

2½ cups white vinegar

1 cup water

6 tablespoons canning salt (don't use any other kind of salt)

4 large cloves garlic

4 large sprigs fresh dill

4 whole red chiles, such as chile de árbol

Sterilize four pint jars and soften four fresh lids in very hot water.

Rinse and dry the green beans, removing any that look bruised. Snap the base off of each bean and keep the delicate top, arranging them in separate piles of long and short ones. Beans that are about 4¼ inches tall will stand perfectly in a pint jar and allow enough head room for safe canning; shorter ones are ideal for filling in the gaps.

Bring the vinegar, water, and canning salt to a simmer in a medium pan. Stir until all of the salt is dissolved; keep warm on low heat.

Break the garlic cloves in half and place 2 halves at the bottom of each jar. Tear the dill sprigs in half. Holding a jar at an angle, lay one piece of dill and one chile along the inside. Fill with green beans, starting with the longer beans and filling in the gaps with the shorter ones. Before the jar is filled, place the other piece of dill on the other side of the jar. Repeat with the other jars. Keep pressing the remaining beans in into each jar. You want a snug fit to avoid floaters.

Pour the hot vinegar mixture over the beans to fill the jars, leaving about 1 inch of head space. Wipe the rims and apply the lids and rings, then process in a water bath for 10 minutes.

Remove the jars to a heatproof surface and cool completely before moving. Store them at room temperature for up to a year in a cool, dark place. Let the mixture to do its work for at least three weeks before eating.

Virginia Willis's Bon Appetit Y'all Green Beans

Virginia Willis is one of the most accomplished southern chefs I know and the author of Bon Appetit Y'all. *Her style of cooking brings together the foodways of the South with the flavors of France, where she lived while attending the La Varenne Cooking School under the tutelage of Anne Willan. Virginia is also a very dear friend of mine, and despite the distance that separates us, our love of food keeps us close. There is nothing we enjoy more than to cook for each other and sit around a family table to enjoy good food whenever we can. This is my adaptation of one of her recipes. She recommends using the best haricots verts that you can find for this recipe, but I find that young Blue Lake beans also work great. When we get together, we blend our cultures at the table. I love these green beans paired with a grilled salmon and creamy grits enhanced with roasted poblano pepper strips and good melting cheese.*

MAKES 4–6 SERVINGS

1 tablespoon salt (plus more, to taste)

1½ pounds haricots verts

2 tablespoons extra-virgin olive oil

1 large clove garlic, minced

2 large plum tomatoes, seeded and chopped

15 pitted Kalamata olives, cut in half

1 tablespoon minced parsley

2 tablespoons minced basil

2 tablespoons red wine vinegar

Freshly ground black pepper, to taste

Fill a large bowl with iced water; set aside. Fill a large pot with water and bring it to a boil over high heat. Add 1 tablespoon of the salt; allow the water to return to a boil. Add the beans and cook until al dente, about 3–4 minutes. Drain and immediately plunge them into the iced water to stop the cooking; cool completely, drain again, and set aside.

Heat the oil in the same pot over low heat. Add the garlic and cook until fragrant, about 45 seconds. Add the haricot verts, tomatoes, olives, parsley, and basil; toss to combine. Add the vinegar and stir well. Season with salt and pepper and serve hot, at room temperature, or chilled.

Pickled Green Beans Escabeche

Perfectly crispy and bright green Blue Lake beans start to make an appearance in early June, and although these are not considered southern beans, they are the most commonly found in grocery stores in the South. I love them cooked and buttered or drenched in vinaigrette. Platters of scantily dressed vegetables are a common sight on southern tables, particularly during the hot summer months, when they are in season. For the most part, cooks give summer vegetables an effortless treatment: tomatoes are simply sliced, corn is just boiled, and young green beans are cooked simply. Here, I quickly pickle them with a classic vinaigrette. If you grow your own beans or frequent farmers' markets, choose the youngest possible green beans that snap when bent.

MAKES 6 SERVINGS

2 pounds green beans (such as Blue Lakes)
¼ cup apple cider vinegar
2 tablespoons Dijon mustard
2 tablespoons finely chopped flat-leaf parsley
¼ cup minced shallots
1 garlic clove, minced
¾ teaspoon salt, or to taste
¼ teaspoon freshly ground black pepper, or to taste
½ cup extra-virgin olive oil

Trim the stem side of the beans, leaving the tips intact. Bring 2 quarts of water to a boil in a large pot over high heat. Fill a bowl with iced water. Drop the beans into the pot and bring the water back to a boil; cook until al dente, about 6–8 minutes. Remove the beans with a slotted spoon and quickly transfer to the iced water; cool for 10 minutes. Drain the beans and set aside.

In a medium bowl, whisk together the vinegar, mustard, parsley, shallots, garlic, salt, and pepper. Slowly whisk in the oil in a thin stream until the dressing becomes creamy.

Toss the beans with the dressing and arrange them on a platter; spoon any remaining dressing over the beans and serve.

Baby Butter Bean Crostini

Few chefs have done more for contemporary southern cuisine than Ben and Karen Barker. Together, at Magnolia Grill, their legendary restaurant in Durham, North Carolina, they treated gourmands to a new style of southern food and soon after introduced it to the world. Their pioneering approach, which celebrated local produce and catapulted the region's farm-to-fork movement, proved that southern cuisine was all grown-up and could be as elegant as any other prized cuisine. They used classic, seasonal southern ingredients in innovative and groundbreaking ways while mentoring a group of chefs that continue to change the way that new southern food is prepared today. I chose this recipe to close this chapter because although, sadly, Magnolia Grill has closed its doors after almost twenty years, the culinary revolution that the Barkers began continues.

MAKES APPROXIMATELY 1 DOZEN

FOR THE BUTTER BEAN PURÉE

2 tablespoons olive oil

¼ cup sliced shallots

1 bay leaf, preferably fresh

8 ounces fresh or frozen butter beans

Approximately 1¾ cups vegetable or chicken stock
   (or enough to cover beans)

2 tablespoons roasted garlic purée (see Note)

Finely grated zest of 2 lemons

2 tablespoons extra-virgin olive oil

¼ cup herbs of your choice, chopped (we like a mixture of
   marjoram, Italian parsley, and basil)

Salt and freshly ground black pepper, to taste

FOR THE CROSTINI
1 baguette, sliced ½ inch thick on a slight bias
¼ cup olive oil
Additional herbs for garnishing

To make the butter bean purée, heat the olive oil in a medium sauté pan. Add the sliced shallots and bay leaf. Sauté the shallots until soft. Add the butter beans and enough stock to just cover them. Bring to a simmer, reduce the heat, and cook until the beans are tender, adding a bit more stock if necessary. Cool completely over an ice bath. Remove the bay leaf.

Roughly purée the butter beans in a food processor, pulsing. Do not overprocess—they should retain a bit of texture. Add the roasted garlic purée, lemon zest, extra-virgin olive oil, herbs, salt, and pepper. Pulse to combine. Refrigerate if not using immediately. Bring to room temperature before assembling the crostini. This is best made shortly before using, as the color has a tendency to turn if prepared too far in advance.

To assemble the crostini, brush the baguette slices with the oil on both sides. Grill or toast the bread until golden brown. Slather it generously with butter bean purée and sprinkle with additional herbs.

NOTE ❋ To make the roasted garlic purée, heat the oven to 350°. Toss the unpeeled cloves of 4 heads of garlic with olive oil, wrap them tightly in foil, and bake for 35–45 minutes or until the garlic is soft. Cool slightly, peel, and purée; cover with a film of olive oil and keep in the refrigerator until ready to use.

International Dishes

Beans and peas are adored around the world and you'll find an endless collection of recipes that could fill an entire encyclopedia on the subject matter. Coming up with recipes to include in this chapter was easy. What was decidedly difficult was selecting my favorites. And that is what I have done here: These are the recipes I like to teach in my classes and that have been lauded by my cooking students for both their practicality and their succulence. You'll find here culinary interpretations from Mexico and Cuba, Greece and Lebanon, Italy and France, among others. I hope that you'll include them in your cooking repertoire, because no matter what language you speak, these recipes always taste good!

Gallo Pinto

The first time I tasted Hoppin' John, I immediately thought of this Central American mélange of rice and beans. Every country in the Americas has at least one recipe that marries rice and beans, but this is one of my favorites. A Nicaraguan churrasco *(their equivalent of a southern pig pickin' but without the pig) will always feature char-grilled beef, plantains, some kind of tomato salsa, and this rice and bean combo. The surprise ingredient here is the Worcestershire sauce, which is used generously; "Worcestershire" is hard for native Spanish speakers to pronounce, so Latin Americans simply call it English sauce. Here, it adds a touch of piquancy to the rice that teases the palate with a little kick of spice that otherwise would be provided by chiles. This is the perfect recipe for that leftover rice from last night's dinner that you don't know what to do with. Try this, and you'll see why Nicaraguans and Costa Ricans vie to claim it as their national dish.*

MAKES 6 SERVINGS

2½ tablespoons vegetable oil
½ cup finely chopped white or yellow onion
½ cup finely chopped green bell pepper
2 cups home-cooked or canned dark-red kidney beans, drained and rinsed
2½ cups cooked white rice
⅓ cup Worcestershire sauce
¼ cup water
Salt and freshly ground black pepper, to taste

In a large sauté pan with high sides, heat the oil over medium-high heat; add the onion and peppers and cook, stirring, until softened, about 2–3 minutes. Add the beans and cook, tossing, for 2–3 minutes (some of the beans will split open, which is fine). Add the rice, Worcestershire sauce, and water, stirring well to coat the rice. Reduce the heat to medium-low and cook until the mixture is heated through, about 5 minutes. Serve immediately.

Black Beans and Broth with Herbed Croutons

Here is a recipe that yields two different things: perfectly cooked beans and a succulent likker that becomes a delicate broth. I cut my teeth on this humble but fortifying soup (and so did my children). Who knew I was drinking pot likker way back when I was a little girl growing up in Guatemala City? Once a week, a pot of beans bubbled away on the stove in my childhood kitchen; with the same frequency, the broth, or caldo, *made its appearance at the table. Black beans produce a dark, blackish-brown likker. For this recipe, I flavor my beans with aromatics and then strain them, saving the liquid. At the end of the process, I have a beautiful batch of delicious cooked black beans, ideal for making any of the recipes in this book that call for beans, such as my Mean Bean Burgers with Chipotle Mayo (page 61), salsas, or salads. In my home, we always serve this with a big basket of crispy homemade croutons. If you wish, stir a cup of the cooked beans back into the broth.*

MAKES 4–6 SERVINGS

FOR THE BROTH

1 pound black beans, soaked overnight and drained

½ large yellow onion, unpeeled

4–6 large garlic cloves, left whole and peeled

1 bay leaf

¼ teaspoon ground cumin

2½ teaspoons salt, or to taste

¼ teaspoon freshly ground black pepper, or to taste

6 slices white sandwich bread, cut into 1-inch squares
¼ cup extra-virgin olive oil
1 tablespoon finely chopped parsley (leaves and tender stems)
1 tablespoon finely chopped cilantro (leaves and tender stems)
2 teaspoons finely chopped chives

Place the beans, onion, garlic, and bay leaf in a 6- to 8-quart Dutch oven. Add enough water to cover the beans by at least 3 inches and bring to a boil over medium-high heat. Cover, reduce the heat to low and simmer until the beans are tender, about 1 hour (older beans will take longer).

To make the croutons, preheat the oven to 350°. In a large bowl toss together the bread, oil, parsley, cilantro, and chives. Spread the bread onto a large baking pan in one layer and bake, tossing once, for 10–15 minutes or until golden and crispy. Transfer the croutons to a basket. (The croutons may be prepared up to 2 hours before serving; cool before storing in a container).

Strain the broth into a large measuring cup remove the onion, garlic, and bay leaf from the beans and discard. Save the beans for another recipe (if covered and chilled, they'll keep up to 1 week).

Add enough water to the broth to make 8 cups of liquid and return it the pot. Add the cumin, salt, and pepper and re-heat it over medium-low heat, about 5–8 minutes. Ladle into bowls and top with croutons; serve extra croutons on the side.

Cuban Black Bean Soup

I have made this soup—one of my family's standby dinners—for years, and, serve it along with chopped avocadoes and white rice. You'll likely find this aromatic and comforting soup prepared in many homes and restaurants in Florida, which is home to many Cuban expats. The roots of the dish may be Cuban, but it has become a staple of southern cuisine. The broth has a deep, rich flavor with a bit of heat, but it isn't too spicy-hot. It's seasoned with sofrito, a Latin American flavor base made with onions and bell peppers, which lends a sweet undertone. This particular sofrito, which gets most of its flavor from green bell peppers, provides the distinct Creole taste of this Caribbean island's culinary culture; it's added at the end of the cooking process so that the flavors remain fresh. This soup tastes better after it sits for a while, so make a large batch and reserve half in the fridge for later in the week. For a thicker soup, double the amount of mashed beans and stir them back into the soup.

MAKES 8–10 SERVINGS

- 1 pound dried black beans, cleaned of debris
- 2 medium yellow onions, 1 halved and the other coarsely chopped, divided
- 2 green bell peppers, 1 cored, seeded, and halved and the other coarsely chopped, divided
- 2 bay leaves
- 4 large garlic cloves, coarsely chopped
- 1 Cuban ajicito chile or jalapeño pepper, seeded and coarsely chopped
- 2 tablespoons extra-virgin olive oil
- 2 teaspoons ground cumin
- 1 teaspoon oregano
- 1½ tablespoons salt
- ½ teaspoon freshly ground black pepper

½ cup white wine
2 tablespoons sherry vinegar
4 cups cooked white rice (optional)

Place the beans in a large bowl and add enough cold water to cover them by at least 2 inches; soak for at least 6 hours or overnight (or use my quick-soak method, page 32). Drain the beans and rinse them under cold water.

Combine the beans and the water. Add the halved onion, the halved bell pepper, and the bay leaves. Bring the liquid to a rolling boil over medium-high heat and boil for 5 minutes, skimming off the foam that rises to the surface; cover, reduce the heat to low, and simmer for 1½–2 hours or until the beans are soft.

When the beans have finished cooking, remove and discard the onion, bell pepper, and bay leaves. Remove one cup of the beans and mash them well. Return them to the pot, stir, and keep warm.

Place the remaining (chopped) onion and bell pepper, the garlic, and the chile in the bowl of food processor fitted with a metal blade; pulse for six 5-second intervals or until they are puréed, stopping to scrape down the sides of the bowl a few times.

Heat the oil in a medium nonstick skillet over medium-high heat. Add the puréed mixture, cumin, oregano, salt, and pepper and cook for 4–5 minutes or until it resembles a paste. Add the wine and vinegar; cooking for 2–3 minutes or until the liquid has evaporated. Pour this into the bean soup and stir well. Bring the soup back to a simmer; cook, covered for 10 minutes. Taste and season with more salt, if needed. Serve in deep bowls with or without rice.

Bean, Avocado, and Roasted Red Pepper Quesadillas

These vegetarian favorites are healthy and satisfying. I make them when I'm feeling lazy and want a quick and easy supper. Use my Classic Refried Pinto or Black Beans (page 100) or your favorite canned version. Select an avocado that yields slightly to the touch and slice it just before assembling the quesadillas or it will blacken. I keep jars of roasted bell peppers in my pantry just so I can make these on a whim. Serve these with your favorite store-bought or homemade salsa.

MAKES 4 SERVING

4 (9-inch) flour tortillas
2 cups canned or homemade refried beans
2 cups shredded Muenster, cheddar, or Monterey Jack cheese
1 roasted red bell pepper, thinly sliced
1 Hass avocado, halved, pitted, peeled, and thinly sliced
1 tablespoon vegetable oil

Place the tortillas flat on a clean cooking surface. Spread half of each tortilla with the beans and top each with ¼ cup of the cheese. Divide the bell pepper among the tortillas, placing the slices over the cheese; do the same with the avocado. Top each with ¼ cup of the remaining cheese. Fold the bare half of each tortilla over the filling.

Preheat a nonstick skillet over medium heat (or heat a griddle to 300°). Brush one side of the quesadillas with the oil; place them, oil side down, on the heated pan. Cook on the first side, rotating them occasionally, for 2 minutes, or until golden. Gently flip them to the other side, being careful not to lose the filling, and cook for another 2–3 minutes or until golden and the cheese has melted. Keep in mind that if the pan or griddle is too hot, the tortillas will burn and the interiors of the quesadillas will remain cold, so monitor them carefully. Reduce the heat if necessary.

Slice each into 2–3 pieces and serve.

NOTE ✳ There is no need to oil both sides of the quesadillas; the oil used on the first side will coat the bottom of the pan before the second side is flipped, making for perfectly crispy quesadillas on both sides.

Classic Refried Pinto or Black Beans

These beans are the most commonly featured side dish in Mexican and Central American cuisine. They're very simple to make and offer a comforting, luscious flavor. These are richly seasoned and fried with lard, but you can use vegetable oil instead. The beans are mashed directly on the skillet using a potato masher as they fry. I love to top these beans with a good melting cheese, such as queso fresco or Monterey Jack, and a touch of sour cream or Mexican crema. For recipes that require a completely smooth bean purée (like the Black Bean Sombreros with Avocado Crema on page 64), simply process the cooked beans until smooth.

MAKES 8 SERVINGS

1 pound dried pinto or black beans, cleaned of debris

$\frac{1}{4}$ large white onion, plus $\frac{1}{2}$ cup minced onion, divided

1 bay leaf

1 large garlic clove, peeled and left whole

$\frac{1}{4}$ cup lard or vegetable oil

$1\frac{1}{2}$ teaspoons salt, or to taste

$1\frac{1}{2}$ cups crumbled queso fresco or shredded
  Monterey Jack cheese

1 cup sour cream (optional)

Place the beans in a large bowl. Add enough water to cover the beans by at least 2 inches; soak for at least 6 hours or overnight (or use my quick-soak method, page 32). Drain the beans and rinse them under cold water.

Place the beans in a large Dutch oven with the piece of onion, the bay leaf, and the garlic; add enough cold water to cover by 2½ inches. Bring the beans to a boil over medium-high heat; cover, reduce the heat, and simmer for 1–1½ hours or until the beans are fork-tender (add more water if needed). Strain the beans over a large bowl and reserve the pot likker. Discard the bay leaf and reserve the onion and the garlic.

In a large frying pan heat the lard over medium-high heat. Add the remaining onion and cook until it begins to turn a golden color, about 2 minutes. Add the beans, the reserved onion and garlic, and the salt. While they cook and using a potato masher, mash them to a consistency of lumpy mashed potatoes, adding 2½ cups of the reserved liquid a little bit at a time, to help you mash them. Heat well and serve, topped with cheese and cream, if desired.

NOTE ✻ If you prefer a thinner consistency, add more liquid while the beans cook; if you prefer them a bit stiffer, continue cooking until they reach the desired consistency. If you're making the beans a day ahead of time, reserve an additional cup of pot likker (or water) to thin out the beans as they're reheated.

The Big Pot of Minestrone

Minestra *is "soup" in Italian, and minestrone means "big soup." This recipe, which originates from Genoa, is one of my favorite vehicles to use the different varieties of beans available in the American South. Adding a dollop of pesto at the end produces a soup that tastes luxurious even though it's not expensive to prepare. Pancetta is Italian rolled pork fat; it's similar to bacon but is cured rather than smoked. (You may substitute bacon in this recipe if you want.) I save the rinds of Parmigiano-Reggiano cheese in the freezer and add one to this simmering soup for added flavor—my secret to great minestrone—but it'll taste sensational without it too! This recipe makes a great big aromatic pot of goodness. Freeze any leftovers for up to 3 months.*

MAKES 12 SERVINGS

- 1 cup dried red kidney beans, cleaned of debris, soaked overnight, and drained, or 2 (14-ounce) cans, drained and rinsed
- 1 cup dried great northern beans, cleaned of debris, soaked overnight and drained, or 2 (14-ounce) cans, drained and rinsed
- 4 quarts chicken broth, or more if needed
- 1 tablespoon olive oil
- 1 cup chopped pancetta
- 1½ cups finely chopped white or yellow onion
- 1½ cups finely chopped carrot
- 1½ cups finely chopped celery
- 2 garlic cloves, minced
- 1 cup red wine (such as Merlot)
- 2 cups chopped zucchini
- 4 cups peeled and diced Russet potatoes
- 1½ cups diced plum tomatoes
- 2 cups broad or pole beans, cut into 1-inch pieces
- ½ cup chopped flat-leaf parsley

2½ teaspoons salt, or to taste
½ teaspoon freshly ground black pepper, or to taste
Rind from a Parmigiano-Reggiano cheese (optional)
1 cup prepared pesto
1½ cups grated Parmigiano-Reggiano or Parmesan cheese,
   or to taste

Place the dried beans in an 8-quart pot; add enough cold water to cover them by 2 inches. Bring to a boil over medium-high heat; boil for 5 minutes, skimming off the foam that rises to the surface. Cover, reduce the heat to low and cook the beans until tender, about 45–60 minutes.

When the beans are ready, strain and return them to the pot (discard the cooking water); add the chicken broth and bring to a simmer over medium-high heat; simmer, uncovered, for 10 minutes.

In a large sauté pan, set over medium-high heat, heat the olive oil and cook the pancetta for 2–4 minutes to render the fat and give it a nice golden color. Add the onions, carrots, and celery and cook, stirring, until softened, about 4–5 minutes. Add the garlic and cook for 30 seconds or until fragrant. Add the wine and stir, scraping up the brown bits from the bottom of the pan, and cook for 1 minute.

Add the cooked vegetables to the pot with the broth and beans. Stir in the zucchini, potatoes, tomatoes, broad beans, and parsley. Add the rind, if using, and the salt and pepper. Bring the soup to a boil, reduce the heat to low, and simmer for 30 minutes. If the soup is too thick, add more broth (or water), until it reaches the desired consistency.

If using, discard the rind. Ladle the soup into bowls; top with a spoonful of pesto, and sprinkle with the grated cheese.

Classic Pasta e Fagiole

I don't believe in making small pots of soup, especially if I'm making one this good. This is my take on the classic stick-to-your-ribs soup. Fagiole *is the Italian word for beans, and although the proper pronunciation of this soup is "pasta eh fah-DJOH-leh," Italian Americans have morphed it into something that sounds more like "pasta eh fah-zool." Cooking the pasta separately and then adding it to the soup prevents the starch from clouding the broth and keeps the pasta from falling apart. Every winter, I invite close friends to a casual party. I make three soups and set plenty of mugs on the counter so everyone can help themselves directly from the steaming pots on my stove. The only other things on the menu are a big salad and crusty artisan bread. This soup is always a crowd favorite. Leftovers can be stored in the refrigerator for up to 4 days, but you'll need to add more broth when reheating it since the pasta will absorb most of it as it sits.*

MAKES 10 SERVINGS

2 teaspoons extra-virgin olive oil

¾ pound pancetta or bacon, chopped

1 cup finely chopped leeks

⅔ cup finely chopped carrots

½ cup finely chopped celery

¼ cup finely chopped shallots

8 large garlic cloves, minced

1 pound cooked cannellini or great northern beans,
   rinsed, drained, and divided

1 (28-ounce) can crushed tomatoes (with liquid)

1 (28-ounce) can whole tomatoes, chopped (with liquid)

10 cups chicken broth, or more, to taste

10 sprigs fresh thyme or 2 teaspoons dried

2 tablespoons chopped fresh oregano or 2 teaspoons dried

2 tablespoons chopped fresh sage or 2 teaspoons dried

1 tablespoon salt, or to taste

½ teaspoon freshly ground black pepper, or to taste

1 pound small pasta such as ditalini or tubetti pasta,
   cooked according package directions

1 cup finely chopped flat-leaf parsley (leaves and
   tender stems)

Grated Parmigiano-Reggiano or Parmesan cheese, to taste

In a large stockpot, heat the oil over medium-high heat; add the pancetta or bacon and cook until it has rendered its fat and is beginning to crisp, about 4 minutes. Remove the pancetta or bacon from the pot, and set it on paper towels to drain. Discard all but 1 tablespoon of the rendered fat.

Return the pot to medium-high heat and add the leeks, carrots, celery, and shallots; cook, stirring, until they begin to soften, about 2–3 minutes. Add the garlic and sauté until fragrant or about 30 seconds. Add the beans, tomatoes, and pancetta and stir well; simmer for 5 minutes. Add the broth, thyme, oregano, sage, salt, and pepper. Bring the soup to a boil; reduce the heat, cover, and simmer for 20 minutes.

Remove 2 cups of the beans, mash them well, and return them to the soup. Add the cooked pasta and simmer for 5 minutes or until the pasta is warmed through.

Ladle the soup into bowls and sprinkle with parsley and cheese.

NOTE ❋ This soup should be on the thick side, but if you prefer it to be looser, then add more broth.

Black-Eyed Pea and Dill Salad

Creamy peas are bathed in a tangy dressing in this colorful rendition of a Greek classic. Black-eyed peas were already popular in the Mediterranean region long before they made it to the American South, and not surprisingly, they're frequently used in recipes such as this refreshing salad. When you make the salad, it should sit at room temperature for about 30 minutes in order for the marinade to penetrate each pea; or make it a couple of days ahead of time and refrigerate it until ready to serve. I like to bring this salad to room temperature before serving and find it's a great accoutrement to grilled fish and seafood, or as part of an antipasti platter.

MAKES 6 SERVINGS

1 pound cooked and drained black-eyed peas (see Note)
1 cup coarsely chopped red onion
2 large garlic cloves, minced
½ cup finely chopped fresh dill (see Note)
½ cup finely chopped flat-leaf parsley (leaves and tender stems)
½ cup fresh lemon juice
2 teaspoons red wine vinegar
1½–2 teaspoons salt, or to taste
¼ teaspoon freshly ground black pepper
¼ teaspoon red pepper flakes
½ cup extra-virgin olive oil

In a large bowl combine the peas, onion, garlic, dill, and parsley. In a small bowl, whisk together the lemon juice, vinegar, salt, pepper, and red pepper flakes; add the oil in a thin stream, whisking constantly until combined. Pour the dressing over the peas and stir well. Let it sit at room temperature, stirring occasionally, for 30 minutes. Serve immediately, or cover and chill for longer storage (up to 3 days).

NOTE ✱ You can also use canned peas; just be sure to rinse and drain them well before using. Make sure to wash the dill in plenty of cold water as it's sometimes full of sand; dry it between towels before chopping or it will blacken.

Acarajés
Black-Eyed Pea Fritters

If you visit Salvador da Bahia, Brazil, you can buy these crunchy black-eyed pea fritters at street stands from women wearing white cotton garb. They beckon passersby with their chant of "acará-je," which means "I have acarás." This recipe can be traced back centuries to Western Africa, where similar bean cakes are still eaten today. In the South, an early colonial recipe for bean fritters can be found in The Virginia Housewife. *These acarajés feature reddish exteriors and dense, creamy, white centers. The recipe calls for peeling the black-eyed peas, and since fresh peas are much easier to peel than dried peas, I make these only during the summer months. Canned peas simply don't work in this recipe because they're too mushy and the fritters won't hold their shape. Start this recipe one day before you plan on serving it so that you have plenty of time to soak the black-eyed peas.*

MAKES 6–7 SERVINGS

---

5 cups fresh or frozen black-eyed peas (see Note)
½ cup grated white or yellow onion, strained to remove juices
3 large garlic cloves, grated
1 teaspoon salt
Vegetable oil for frying (see Note)

Place the peas in a large bowl, cover with cold water, soak for at least 12 hours or overnight in the refrigerator. Drain and, working in batches, rub them between 2 kitchen towels until they split in half and their skins come off. Pick out the peas and transfer them to a bowl of cold water; discard the skins. Soak the peas for 2 hours and drain.

Place the peas in a sturdy blender. Add enough water to get the motor running (start with 1–1¼ cups); pulse for 5-second intervals until the peas are smooth and feel like soft mashed potatoes—the purée must hold its shape when pressed between the fingers. If the peas are too watery, drain them through a sieve lined with a kitchen towel. If the mixture is too dry, add a bit more water.

Transfer the puréed peas to a stand mixer fitted with the paddle attachment. Add the onion, garlic, and salt; whip on medium speed for 2 minutes (or whip by hand with a spatula for 3 minutes). On low speed, whip for 2 more minutes or until the peas are light and fluffy (or whip by hand for 5 minutes).

Fit a large baking pan with a metal cooling rack. In a medium pot, heat 2–3 inches of oil to 350° (or use a deep fryer according to the manufacturer's directions). To test the batter for the proper consistency, press a tablespoon of the mixture into a ball and drop it in the oil. If it falls apart, the batter is too wet; drain again. If it sinks to the bottom and sticks to the pan, whip the rest of the batter for a few more minutes.

Working with one acarajé at a time, scoop up ½ cup of the pea batter with a large spoon; transfer the batter to a second large spoon, using the spoon to scrape it out of the first spoon, yielding a football shape (or quenelle). Carefully, slide the batter into the oil. It should sink briefly and float to the top. Repeat with the rest of the batter. Fry the fritters for 3½–4½ minutes, turning them over halfway through, until both sides are a reddish-brown color. Use a slotted spoon to transfer them to the prepared rack to drain.

NOTE ✽ If you want to use dried peas for this recipe, soak them for 3–4 days in the refrigerator to enable their skins to come off. These are traditionally fried in dendé (red palm oil), but it is very high in saturated fat, so I avoid using it. You can make these into smaller fritters and serve them as hors d'oeuvres; adjust the cooking time as necessary.

Puerto Rican Rice and Pigeon Peas

This symphony of rice and peas gets its gutsy taste from a mixture of aromatics called recaíto—*which is easily made in a food processor—and with annatto. This flavor base that's enriched by the flavor of* culantro—*a long, leafy herb that tastes like uber cilantro—is sold in jars or in the frozen section of many grocery stores around the United States. I include the recipe for homemade* recaíto *here, in case you have access to fresh culantro and prefer to make it yourself. You'll need only half of the* recaíto *to make this recipe (it makes 1 cup) and can freeze the other half for up to 6 months, so you can whip up this dish easily a second time around. Pigeon peas are a staple of the African American soul food movement, and they're the most popular pea used by cooks in Miami.* Arroz con gandúles *is Puerto Rico's national dish, usually reserved for special occasions and typically served up with fried pork chunks* (masitas de puerco) *or a whole roast leg of pork* (pernil). *Make sure to sauté the rice exactly as directed so that it can absorb the annatto color before you add any liquid or it won't take the uniform, golden color that defines this dish.*

MAKES 8 SERVINGS

FOR THE RECAÍTO
1½ cups yellow onion, roughly chopped
1 green bell pepper, seeded, cored, and roughly chopped
1½ cups roughly chopped culantro (leaves and tender stems)
1½ cups chopped cilantro (leaves and tender stems)
2 Cuban ajíes or jalapeño peppers, seeded and deveined
3 large garlic cloves, roughly chopped
¼ cup extra-virgin olive oil

FOR THE RICE
½ cup extra-virgin olive oil
1 tablespoon annatto seeds
½ cup homemade or store-bought recaíto

2 cups long-grain white rice
4 cups chicken broth or water
½ pound cooked pigeon peas, drained
2 teaspoons salt, or to taste
¼ teaspoon freshly ground black pepper, or to taste
1 large banana leaf, cut to fit the top of the pot

To make the recaíto, in the bowl of a food processor fitted with a metal blade, combine the onion, bell pepper, culantro, cilantro, ajíes, and garlic; pulse 15–20 times for 3-second intervals or until finely chopped, stopping to scrape down the sides of the bowl, as needed.

Heat ¼ cup of the oil in a 10-inch skillet over medium-high heat. Add the processed mixture and cook, stirring, until thick, about 5–6 minutes. Cool completely. Set ½ cup aside; freeze the rest in an airtight container for up to 6 months.

To make the rice, in a small saucepan, combine the remaining ¼ cup of oil with the annatto seeds over medium heat. As soon as the oil begins to bubble (it'll take about 1 minute), remove the pan from the heat and let the seeds steep for 10 minutes; strain and discard the seeds.

Transfer the oil to a 5- to 6-quart Dutch oven and heat it over medium-high heat. When the oil is hot, add the reserved ½ cup of recaíto and cook for 30 seconds or until fragrant. Add the rice and stir well; cook, stirring vigorously, for 2 minutes (being careful not to burn it). Add the broth or water and bring to a rolling boil; add the peas, salt, and pepper. Cover the pot with the banana leaf and bring the liquid back to a boil; cover the pot with a tight-fitting lid and reduce the heat to low; simmer the rice for 18–22 minutes or until all of the liquid has been absorbed. Discard the banana leaf before serving.

Butter Bean Risotto

This creamy, hearty, and comforting rice dish is my take on the Venetian classic called risi e bisi, *usually made with green English peas. Butter beans, with their velvety texture and beautiful pale-green color, make a great addition to risotto. I particularly appreciate being able to use these, long after fresh English peas have disappeared from the market stalls. Not only do they keep their shape as they cook, but their nutty flavor complements that of the other ingredients featured in this recipe. Risotto is quite easy to master once a few basics are understood. The most important is to use the proper type of rice, and here, Arborio, Carnaroli, or Vialone Nanno, which are all short-grain, Italian rice varieties, will work. Risotto is valued for its creaminess, obtained by stirring the rice as it cooks while adding liquid in small increments, so that the grains can slowly release the starchy compound—known as amylopectin—resulting in a luxurious consistency. Arborio rice is the easiest variety to find and, in my experience, produces a delicious thick and creamy texture. I serve this risotto on late summer days paired with a green salad and a glass of cold white wine.*

MAKES 6 SERVINGS

2 tablespoons unsalted butter

1 tablespoon extra-virgin olive oil

½ cup finely chopped Vidalia onion

1½ cups Arborio rice

½ cup white wine

6 cups hot chicken or vegetable broth

½ pound cooked and drained butter beans

1 cup grated Parmigiano-Reggiano or Parmesan cheese

1 teaspoon salt, or to taste

¼ teaspoon white pepper, or to taste

Combine the butter and the oil in a medium pot and heat over medium-high heat until the butter is melted. Add the onion and cook, stirring, until translucent, about 1–2 minutes. Add the rice, and cook, stirring, until it's well coated with the oil and butter and the grains turn opaque, about 30 seconds. Add the wine and stir vigorously until it evaporates, about 30 seconds. Reduce the heat to medium, add ½ cup of the broth, and stir constantly until it's been absorbed completely, about 30 seconds. Add another ½ cup of broth and continue stirring until all of the liquid has been absorbed, about 30 seconds. Continue adding the broth in ½-cup increments, stirring constantly, adding more broth only when the previous addition has been absorbed by the rice. When you have only 1 cup of broth left, add it all at once; add the butter beans and stir until the rice is al dente and creamy (not soupy but still a bit wet). Stir in the cheese, salt, and pepper, and serve immediately.

NOTE ❊ If the heat is too high, the rice will absorb the liquid too quickly but will remain raw inside. The whole process should take about 18–20 minutes from start to finish.

Lebanese Green Beans with Tomatoes
Loubia B'zeit

You'll find this succulent green bean stew served all over the Middle East and the Mediterranean region, with some slight variations. It's reminiscent of southern stewed beans and tomatoes but is slightly sweeter. It's best made with the very freshest produce at the height of the summer season and the finest extra-virgin olive oil you can find. Select young and crispy green beans that will retain their shape as they cook because they'll have to simmer for a long time. Pick the ripest, juiciest tomatoes you can find or use canned tomatoes, as these will provide the liquid that the beans will simmer in. You'll need a large skillet or a medium pot with a tight-fitting lid for this recipe. I usually serve it over steamed couscous. It's delicious hot or at room temperature.

MAKES 4–6 SERVINGS

⅓ cup extra-virgin olive oil

3 cups finely chopped white onion

1½ pounds green beans (such as Blue Lakes), trimmed

3 large garlic cloves, minced

1½ pounds chopped tomatoes (about 4 heaping cups)

2 tablespoons fresh lemon juice

1 teaspoon sugar

1 teaspoon salt, plus more, to taste

Freshly ground black pepper, to taste

¼ cup finely chopped flat-leaf parsley (leaves and tender stems)

2 tablespoons finely chopped mint (optional)

Heat the oil in a 12-inch skillet over medium-high heat; add the onions and cook, stirring, until softened, about 4–5 minutes. Add the beans and the garlic and reduce the heat to medium; cook until the beans begin to soften, about 4–5 minutes. Add the tomatoes, lemon juice, sugar, salt, and pepper, stirring well. Bring to a boil; cover, reduce the heat to low, and simmer slowly for 35–40 minutes. Check the seasoning and add more salt, if needed. Transfer the beans to a platter. Right before serving, sprinkle with the parsley and mint, if using. Serve hot or at room temperature.

Salade Niçoise My Way

Salade Niçoise is one of the most famous composed salads in the world. The green beans play a supporting role to all of the other ingredients. My husband and I began our honeymoon trip with a week-long stay in Nice, France, were we ordered plenty of salads similar to this one. We tried so many different variations that we felt like experts. We found this one to be one of our favorites, and every summer we re-create it at home. Most recipes for this Provençal salad are made with canned tuna, but I prefer to substitute fresh tuna whenever I can. I serve this one on a large platter, each ingredient separate from the other, so that everyone can get as much of each element as they want, but it's equally beautiful served in individual portions.

MAKES 4 SERVINGS

¾ pound baby white or golden potatoes

½ pound green beans, trimmed

2 large heirloom tomatoes, cut into wedges

1 cup Niçoise olives

¼ cup white wine vinegar

1 tablespoon Dijon mustard

Salt, to taste

Freshly ground black pepper, to taste

½ cup extra-virgin olive oil

8 large basil leaves cut into thin strips (chiffonade)

1 tablespoon minced fresh oregano

2 (6–8 ounce) tuna steaks, preferably ½–1 inch thick

2 teaspoons vegetable oil

2 hard-boiled eggs, peeled, quartered, and chilled

Place the potatoes in a large pot filled with cold water and bring to a boil over medium-high heat. Boil for 20–30 minutes or until fork-tender. Drain the potatoes and rinse them under cold water; peel, quarter, and set them aside.

Bring a large pot of water to a boil and fill a large bowl with iced water. Add the green beans to the boiling water and cook until tender but still al dente (they should retain a bit of crisp). Immediately drain and drop them into the iced water; let them cool completely and then drain.

Arrange the potatoes, green beans, tomatoes, and olives decoratively on a large platter.

In a medium bowl, whisk together the vinegar and mustard and season with salt and pepper. Slowly add the olive oil in a thin stream, whisking as you go, until the dressing has emulsified; stir in the basil and oregano. Reserve 2 tablespoons of the dressing and pour the rest over the salad. Let the salad sit at room temperature while you cook the tuna (up to 30 minutes).

Clean the tuna, making sure to remove any bloody spots; rinse it under cold water and dry well with paper towels. Brush the tuna on both sides with 1 teaspoon of the vegetable oil and season it on both sides with salt and pepper. Heat an outdoor (or indoor) grill until very hot. Brush the grates of the grill with the remaining teaspoon of oil and arrange the tuna steaks on the grill. Cook for 2 minutes; turn the steaks 45 degrees to create nice markings and cook another 2 minutes. Turn the tuna steaks over and cook them on the second side for 2 minutes for rare or 4 minutes for medium-rare (or longer, if desired).

Transfer the tuna steaks to a cutting board and let them rest for 3 minutes. Cut them each on the bias into 6 or 8 slices and place them decoratively on the platter; drizzle the reserved dressing over the tuna, arrange the hard-boiled eggs around the platter, and serve immediately.

VOLUME EQUIVALENTS FOR ONE POUND OF PEAS OR BEANS

I always weigh peas and beans before using them in a recipe, but if you don't have a kitchen scale, the following will be helpful.

Baby lima beans (white or green) (dried)	2 cups
Black or navy beans (dried)	2 cups
Black-eyed peas (fresh)	3 cups
Butter beans (fresh) (1 pound)	3 cups
Butter beans (fresh) (½ pound)	2 cups
Dixie Lee peas (fresh)	2 cups
Emily Lee peas (fresh)	3 cups
Field peas (dried)	2½ cups
Great northern beans (dried)	2 cups
Pink-eyed peas (fresh)	3 cups
Pinto beans (dried)	2¼ cups
Purple crowders (fresh)	3 cups
Red beans (dried)	2 cups
Six-week peas (dried)	2½ cups
Speckled butter beans (dried)	2 cups
Speckled butter beans (fresh)	3 cups
White acre peas (fresh)	2 cups
Yellow-eyed peas (dried)	2 cups

Acknowledgments

I would like to thank Elaine Maisner, my editor and good friend, for inviting me to write about a subject that is close to my heart and for including me as part of the Savor the South collection. I would also like to express my sincere thanks to the entire University of North Carolina Press team for our years of work together.

My deepest thanks go to my husband, Luis, and to our daughters, Alessandra and Niccolle, for their unwavering love and support of my work, and for loving the fact that we ate beans and peas nonstop for one whole year. I wish to give heartfelt thanks to my agent and dear friend Lisa Ekus for her mentorship and steadfast friendship and for always being enthusiastic about my work. Also, my very special appreciation goes to everyone at The Lisa Ekus Group.

I am very grateful to my friends Nathalie Dupree, Nancie McDermott, Marcie Cohen-Ferris, and Bill Ferris for inspiring me one day over breakfast to look beyond the obvious when it came to the subject of this book, so that I could best do it justice.

Many thanks go to author and food historian Ken Albala, author Ronni Lundy, Dr. David Shields from the University of South Carolina, and Dr. Randy Sparks from Tulane University for patiently answering my questions, for sharing their research with me, and for guiding my own research so that I could tell the real story behind southern peas.

My sincere thanks to friends who shared their own special recipes with me: Elizabeth Wiegand, Perre Coleman Magness, Fred Sauceman, Virginia Willis, Nancie McDermott, and Jill Warren Lucas. Thanks also to my fellow UNC Press authors whose recipes I also include in this book: Ben and Karen Barker, Mildred Council, Sallie Ann Robinson, Marcie Cohen-Ferris, Fred Thompson, and the late Bill Neal.

I wish to thank the farmers throughout the South, and especially in Moore County, the Sandhills area of North Carolina, for keeping southern produce alive and well for present and future generations to enjoy, for growing the heirloom legumes that distinguish the American South from every other region in the world, and for always growing the great produce that allowed me to test my recipes seasonally. I'm particularly thankful to my friend A. J. and her family at Andrew's Farm Produce in Mt. Gilead, North Carolina, for making sure that I always had the most beautiful peas and beans while I was working on this project. Thanks also to the folks at the Raleigh Farmers' Market and to the folks at Wise Farms in Mt. Olive, North Carolina.

Thank you, God, for blessings received.

Index